Dean C. Gardner

authorHOUSE

AuthorHouse™
1663 Liberty Drive
Bloomington, IN 47403
www.authorhouse.com
Phone: 833-262-8899

Published by AuthorHouse 11/26/2021

ISBN: 978-1-6655-4605-8 (sc)
ISBN: 978-1-6655-4607-2 (e)

Print information available on the last page.

This book is printed on acid-free paper.

CONTENTS

Dedicated to the way, the Truth and the life.

INTRODUCTION

One of the messages from the 60's was that art and theater, including all of written literature were dead; consequently, it was proposed that there would be a rise of postmodernism. Both prose and poetry joined the no longer. The advance of postmodernism required a new view of what literature was meant to be. Where modernism was grounded in psychology and the portrayal of characters, postmodernism was grounded in the interaction of concepts as the rubric of phenomenology from Hegel, Husserl, Heidegger, and onto the literary theory of Derrida, Foulcoult, Merleau Ponty, Levi-Straus as well as other theorists of post WW2.

Prose was murdered by the rise of pulp fiction with emphasis upon entertainment value. Prose also was the predecessor of video games by allowing the reader to experience the virtual reality of the text. So, the reader used that virtual reality as an escape from existential being. Art had become the opiate of readers leading to a quick fix for the confrontation of what was there.

Poetry experienced another type of death. For the most part, rhyme died from exhaustion.

Other forms of poetry became more narcissistic, confessional dribble of the rehashed and the stroking of the ego. However, there were a small number of poets of intense conceptual content, including Ezra Pound, T.S. Elliot and Wallace Stevens. These few returned the integrity to poetry by teaching critical thinking skills. Of course, the multicultural influence also fed into the rubric of postmodernism with a strong factor from Japan, i.e. the haiku of Basho, Bucson, and Issa. It should be noted that in this era of general collapse, music flourished.

So, postmodern literature pulled from the distant past to resurrect literature from the ash heap; hence, the pRoem, a return to the form of Beowulf, The Canterbury Tales, etc. In this sense, the pRoem is long narrative poetry. Early contemporary efforts show Howl by Ginsberg and The Four Quartets by Elliot, The Cantos by Pound as adequate forerunners of the form of postmodern literature. From the traditional haiku poets the play of juxtaposition and connectivity resulting in a Zen experience offers an essential component in postmodern fiction. Similar to the Zen experience is the crux of Western imagists, where idea next to another offered a poetic leap. Emily Dickinson is a good example of employing the poetic leap in her work. Another feature of postmodern fiction is the emphasis on matters of conceptualization, where ideas play against other ideas and their interaction rather than character development.

Fundamental to postmodern fiction is the emphasis on probing and questioning as the mode to explore phenomenon as the plot of the work. Postmodern literature is there not to entertain but is there to explore and teach. Postmodern fiction releases the bondage of bad faith by uncovering the role of the author. The role of the author of the work surfaces as a voice of the close at hand to shatter the illusion of virtual reality and by so doing leads to the exhaustion of phenomenal reality. From a structural point of view, postmodern fiction uses stanzas rather than paragraphs and each stanza consists of the sentence as the operative mode and elemental building block of progression and flow.

SECTION 1

DAWN OF THE HERE AND NOW

So
It is that unidentified
Flying objects
Are considered
A mystery of life
But Annabel Lee knew
What they are
Through visions cast
While she meditated.

She came to live
In the peace
Beyond understanding
As her trances took her
Into the deep touch
Of The Spirit of Wisdom.

Following the way
The Truth and the life
That connection opened
Her perception
And understanding
Of hidden meaning.

It is
That the ancient Greeks
Called UFOs
The various gods
Led by Zeus.

It is
That the Hindus
Documented the affairs
Of the gods in The Vedas.

Annabel Lee found
That these references
Could be understood
As principalities
Described in The Bible.

So
Annabel Lee came
To understand these UFOs
As the figures
In the war of principalities.

*

In the abundance
Of blooms
The scarlet rose
Spoke to the heart
Of being toward Truth
And the trumpets
Of the always already there
Announced the reading
Of hidden meaning.

It was
The disclosure
Of a reality
Far beyond the rubric
Of being and time.

It was
The unearthing
Of the angels of heaven
And the fallen angels
As their lore determined
The destiny of the world.

Appearing as an old man
Sitting beneath
A banyan tree
An angel of heaven revealed
The treasures of being and time.

Then
The Spirit of Wisdom
Anointed Annabel Lee
And her inner eye saw
The Truth of the plague.

So
The plague that afflicted
The here and now
Was the dark magic
Of fallen angels

As a multitude
From across the planet
Suffered and died.

It was
A ruthless act
By an evil source
That schemed to rule
The world.

How
The people suffered
As nations staggered
Beneath the weight
Of the pandemic.

*

She learned the ways
Of the UFO's
Through her trances
As thoughts eclipsed
The moon
As the dawn chased
The stars away.

It was
The sense of a pure heart
In tune with the rhythm
Of the universe that gathered

The mystery of life
Into images of pure music.

So
She listened
To the songs
Of the wilderness
Revealing hidden meaning
As the angels of heaven
Erased dark magic
As they opened
Her inner eye
To Truth.

It was
Through the looking glass
Of time and space
That allowed Annabel Lee
To witness the activities
Of the principalities
As the war continued.

So
There were three spirits
Two of dark magic
And one that esteemed
Lady Liberty
Two of tyranny
And one of freedom.

In a world of spirits
These three nations
Defined times and a half
That would determine
The destiny of the planet.

So
The world was the battlefield
For the principalities.

So
The UFO's were the signature
Of the angels of heaven
While dark magic ruled the hearts
Of the power hungry
The fallen angels.

*

Wandering through the desert
She came upon living water
Where the scarlet rose
Danced in the gentle
Of a breeze.

It was
Where being toward Truth
Preserved freedom
And the splendor
Of the earth blossomed

In the heart
Of being and nothingness.

How
The song of pure music
Engaged the mind
With The Spirit of Wisdom
As Annabel Lee climbed
Into images
Of awesome wonder.

Escaping the brutality
Of a world sold into madness
She left the despair
Of being and nothingness
Traveling through visions
Of hopes and dreams
And the tyranny
Of the puppet masters
Had no hold on her.

As the world tried
To cancel freedom
Lady Liberty armed
The children of promise
With the way, the Truth
And the life
And legion upon legion
Of angels of heaven
Fortified the here and now.

It is
That the scarlet rose
Is the signature
Of The Unknown God
As the blood of freedom
Drowns the schemes
Of the demigods.

So
Annabel Lee wonders
If peace will
Be given a chance.

Perhaps
Not in this lifetime.

*

As pure music
Perfumed the air
With images
From the other side
Of time and space
The UFO's
Connected to the scarlet rose
And eternity bestowed
Truth across the minds
Of the children of promise.

It was
The Spirit of Wisdom
That launched the deep touch
Into being toward Truth
speaking
The rhythm of the universe
Into the here and now.

As the language
Of being and nothingness
As the language of despair
Wounded the living moment
Thoughts centered upon the way
The Truth and the life
And the drums of eternity
Carried the children of promise
Into life, liberty
And the pursuit of happiness.

How
The echoes of Truth
Established the connection
To the angels of heaven
As the UFO's watched
Over the blue planet.

From the deceit of refuse
Puppet masters conjured
Their rise to power
Through dark magic

But the scarlet rose
With Lady Liberty
Fought against their deception.

So
The power mongers
Twisted language
Concocting their rubric
And defying the authority
Of The Unknown God.

So
There was the war of ideation.

*

As she pursued the unknown
Through her trance
Hidden meaning surfaced
To her inner eye
Triggering being toward Truth
To digest endless possibility.

So
The unidentified
Flying objects
Connected Annabel Lee
To the substance
Of time and space
Through the dance

Of the scarlet rose
While she rode
The rhythm
Of the universe
To what matters.

Leaving the absurdity
Of a world
Sold into madness
She stretched herself
Into a parabola of time
And the image
Of the authentic article
Appeared in a valley
Of quiet waters.

It was
A call in the living moment
That indwelled purpose
Into the chambers of want
And Annabel Lee grasped
The mystery of life.

Orchestrating
The dance of the scarlet rose
Onto a two-dimensional reality
She gathered the winds
Of eternity for the destiny
Of the children of promise.

So
Her trance taught her
To live and let live
As the children of promise
Inherited the crown of Truth.

*

Then
In the garden
Of tables and chairs
The artist pictured
The house of many mansions
And the destiny
Of the scarlet rose
Stepped out of the unknown.

As his vision stirred
An awesome wonder
Into the minds
Of the children of promise
The scarlet rose eclipsed
Being and time
And the thunder
Of being toward Truth
Shook the dull round
Into an awakening.

It was
The rhythm

Of the universe
That he felt in the flow
Of endless possibility
As the scarlet rose defined
The course of action.

Following the authentic article
Of The Spirit of Wisdom
The artist painted freedom
Into the here and now
As the courage
Of human dignity braved
A whole new world.

Because the advance
Of Lady Liberty
Could not be stopped
The fallen angels escaped
To their private hell
The destiny of all tyrants.

So
The UFO's noted
The artist's dance
With the scarlet rose.

*

It was
The deep touch of trance

That brought the mystery of life
Through pure music
To an old man
As his mind drifted
In the warm of the rhythm
Of the universe
Although his inner eye
Registered the chill of despair
In being and nothingness.

Standing before the deception
Of clever language
He weighed the gravity
Of the living moment.

Then
He heard Truth radiate
Across the here and now
Dissolving the false doctrine
Of those with a lust
For power.

Then
Angels of heaven left
A trace to hope
As the world rejected
The purpose of unidentified
Flying objects.

So
The way, the Truth and the life
Infused the experiential
With the authentic article.

As the old man looked
Across the ages
Truth took his meditation
Into the substance
Of what matters.

Although the fallen angels
Tried to cancel his life
The Spirit of Wisdom fortified
His existence
With the dynamics of UFO's.

Then
The Unknown God
Flexed the muscle
Of the old man's faith.

*

Basking in the light
Of The Spirit of Wisdom
Feeding upon the manna
Of the authentic article
The artist reached
Into the heart

Of being toward Truth
Rubbing life
Into the living moment.

There was
The rhythm of the universe
Driving passion into his skull
As an image formed
In the negative space
Of being and nothingness.

Then
Angels of heaven pulled
That image into his mind
And the mystery of life
Birthed pure music.

It was
A rhapsody of forms
Dancing upon the landscape
Of mind.

It was
The breath of eternity
Whispering Truth
Through the wind.

Then
Linear time and space
Conformed to a parabola of time

And a portal to the unknown
Allowed the artist access
To hidden meaning
And Annabel Lee left
The grave of despair.

As the scarlet rose danced
A concept into his mind
Thoughts colored
What was there with the blood
Of forevermore.

So
The UFO's unveiled
The mystery of life
Through the way, the Truth
And the life.

So
The Unknown God smiled.

*

She is a monument
To Truth and justice
As she walks
Through being and time
As she marches
Into mortal combat.

She is
A powerful anthem
Indwelling joy
And wonder in her heart
As she lives a life
Of pure music
As her mind registers
The Spirit of Wisdom.

Facing the madness
Of the world
She wears the breastplate
Of kindness
As her brainwaves
Penetrate the darkness
As her brain waves
Penetrate the darkness
Of ignorance
As she rules out
Pride and prejudice.

So
She dances with angels
Of heaven
Mindful of the place
For unidentified
Flying objects.

So
She embraces being

Toward Truth
As her experiential energy
Encounters phenomenal
Reality
As she follows the way
The Truth and the life
Through the wilds of thought.

Consequentially
Tyrants fear her look
And puppet masters
Tremble.

So
This is Annabel Lee
And Lady Liberty
And the scarlet rose
In the presence
Of The Unknown God.

*

Proceeding from the ashes
Of civilization
Rising above being
And nothingness
The scarlet rose breathed in
The experiential energy
Of the always already there
As she connects

To the artist
Through brain waves.

It is
The activity
Of unidentified
Flying objects that traces
Truth into the hearts
Of the children of promise.

Then
The fragrance
Of the deep touch
Endows the living moment
With the brain waves
Of forevermore
As the scarlet rose
Dances freedom
Into the here and now.

Then
The children of promise
Feel the experiential energy
Of pure music
As The Spirit of Wisdom
Indwells within them.

From across the abyss
A solitary raven carries
An olive branch

Of Truth and justice
And the sacrifice
Of the way, the Truth
And the life awakens
The children of promise
To the land of milk and honey.

It is
The dream of the artist
That blossoms life, liberty
And the pursuit of happiness
Allowing being toward Truth
To rise from the ashes
Of civilization.

So
The will of The Unknown God
Endures onto forevermore.

*

So
The raven spoke
The language of eternity
Into the wind
Unveiling Truth
To those who hear
As the brain waves
Of the always already there

Filled time
And times and a half.

It was
A message of freedom
That all feathered spirits
Of the air echoed
Across all and everything.

They taught
The secrets of the universe
To the scarlet rose
Because of her love
Tried and true.

Unwavering, the raven
Was an ambassador
Of unidentified
Flying objects
As his message declared
Nevermore to the demigods.

So
The good news
Of Truth and justice
Came upon the world
With sudden calm.

As the blood of Truth
Poured into the seas

From rivers of hope
The scarlet rose danced
Her way into victory
Over puppet masters.

Tyrants trembled
As they hid in the abyss
Of their own making.

So
Life returned to the living moment
As Lady Liberty raised the flag
Of freedom forevermore
And the fragrance
Of her scent Filled the air
With brain waves.

*

Teetering on the edge
Of time and space
As a bomb specialist
Who served NYPD
An old man looked
Into the bowels of destiny
As a moon of blood
Rose in the darkness.

As time and times
And a half passed

He answered the call
Of the wilds
Pulling him into the dawn
Of nothingness.

It was
Terror that peeked adrenalin
In the heart of his life
As he faced what was there
With raw courage.

Taking the sword of Truth
He vanquished
The evil before him.

Upon leaving the blast
Of fear, he walked back
To the love
Of the scarlet rose
All in a day's work.

Although the old man
Tasted his death, he configured
Himself outside of the grip
Of the puppet masters
Those who dared to destroy
Freedom.

The dark magic of the demigods
Was no match

For the old man's faith
In the way, the Truth
And the life
As the morning brought
The embrace of his love
The scarlet rose.

Together, they knelt
Before the altar
Of The Unknown God
Where The Spirit of Wisdom
Infused them with clear minds
And pure hearts.

So
There was nothing
To the bomb scare.

Once a bomb specialist
Always a bomb specialist
When duty calls.

*

Awakening in the dark
With the thunder of bombs
Bursting overhead
The old man was consumed
By memories.

There was the cruel pain
To the moment.

Falling into the shadows
Of war
His mind broke.

As he felt the cries
Of buddies with their flesh
Scattered across the terrain
The old man's thoughts
Could not escape
From the war.

So
Life dangled by a thread
Of desolation.

So
The old man could not
Forget his internment
In the pit of hell.

How
He suffered in the cavities
Of desperation
As he looked into the eyes
Of dread.

It was
The ruthless grip
Of war
That pounded his heart
Into nothingness
After time and times
And a half vanquished
The living moment.

Then
He cried out
To The Unknown God
For help.

*

It was
The love of The Unknown God
That taught her
The peace beyond understanding
As the way, the Truth
And the life opened her inner eye
To The Spirit of Wisdom.

So
She experienced the deep touch
Through meditation
As she focused on the song
Of forevermore
And pure music reached

Into her right temple
To the tenderness of her soul.

Riding the rhythm
Of the universe
Her mind tasted
The succulent fruit
Of Truth and justice
As her heart followed
The beat of the drums
Of eternity.

It was
Becoming being toward Truth
That trumpeted her life
Into the living moment
As she conquered
The savage madness
Of a world that sold itself
Into dark magic.

As time and times
And a half multiplied Truth
In her vision
She penetrated
The mystery of life
Grasping the hidden meaning
Of the here and now.

So
She is the twin beam
Of an old man
Onto the always already
There.

*

Although the world did not
Know the artist, the wind
Called him The crystal crow
As he painted his way
Into eternity.

Annabel Lee loved him
Because he had a pure heart.

Together, they danced
In the moonlight
As they followed the stars
Into a wilderness of wonder
And there
They built an altar
To The Unknown God.

As visions rose
In his inner eye
He painted the smile
Of the scarlet rose
And Truth formed

A bridge of prayers
Onto the always
Already there.

It was
A passage of love
That they treasured
As The crystal crow pyramided
Into the moonlight
As Annabel Lee followed him
Into the deep touch
Of the way, the Truth
And the life.

So
They were blessed
With two sons
And three daughters
That grew into pure music
Dedicated to The Spirit
Of Wisdom
And the world listened
To their song.

As the children of promise
That family celebrates freedom
Truth and justice
Across the here and now.

*

Focusing on the moment
When the mockingbird
Embraced time and times
And a half with a song
Brilliant in its way
Annabel Lee left time present
For a parabola of time
As the artist composed
Eternity in a grain of sand.

There was
The beauty of her form
Dancing freedom into the wind.

There was
The other side of the sky
In her substance
That exploded linear
Time and space
Into the frame
Of a two-dimensional reality
As the mockingbird
Opened the look
Of treasures beyond measure.

Then
The groans of the no longer
Summoned angels of heaven
From beyond being and time.

Then
Unidentified flying objects
Crossed the center of thought
Allowing Annabel Lee to harness
The rhythm of the universe
With her smile.

So
The artist meditated
His vision
Into a composition
Between the song
Of the mockingbird
And the dash
Of angels of heaven
As he painted the radiance
Of pure music
Into a portrait of the scarlet rose
Forevermore.

*

It was
War on the home front
When fallen angels
Had infiltrated across the land
Exerting power
Over the minds that stood
For life, liberty and the pursuit
Of happiness.

It was
Through brain waves
That the enemy sought
To dominate and destroy
Those dedicated to the way
The Truth, and the life.

So
Upon a moment
While the artist
Was out and about
That a fallen angel
Invaded his thoughts.

The crystal crow rebuked
The evil for trespassing
Upon his mind.

Then
The fallen angel attacked him
Through brain waves
With the intent
Of giving The crystal crow
A heart attack.

It was
A brutal assault
With measured intent
But The crystal crow battled back.

Although the artist
Was a peaceful sort
He knew that the power
Of dark magic was no match
For The Spirit of Wisdom.

Because The Unknown God
Knew the face of The crystal crow
A legion of angels from heaven
Countered the attack.

So
This evil had
A cerebral hemorrhage
And was directed
To the second death
In the lake of fire
Forevermore
With no chance to escape.

*

SECTION 2

THE CENTER OF THINGS IN THEMSELVES

Strengthening her bond
To the unknown
She traced a connection
To unidentified flying objects
By a leap of faith
And endless possibility
Pictured them
As angels of heaven.

There was
A history of principalities
In the here and now
That allowed her
To see through hidden meaning
To behold this mystery
Of life.

Meditating on The Spirit
Of Wisdom, she gathered
The brain waves
Of the always already there
Into images of Truth
And the thunder of the inevitable
Exploded her thoughts.

Then
Her vision encompassed
The elements
Of what matters
As pure music

Synchronized her mind
To the rhythm of the universe
As brain waves brought
Truth into the living moment.

It was
Through the brain waves
Of the scarlet rose
That she worked her way
Onto being toward Truth
As the integrity
Of the human spirit
Energized her connection
To the UFO's.

So
She trusted her sensibility
Allowing her to dance
With the angels of heaven.

*

Basking in the light
Of a body of Truth
Annabel Lee launches
Into the unknown
As her trance connects
To the authentic article
And being toward Truth
Follows the rhythm

Of the universe
Into hidden meaning.

There is the sweet perfume
Of hope in the garden
Of tables and chairs
As she buries shadows
Of being and nothingness.

Willing herself into the life
Of the scarlet rose
She listens to the pure music
Of The Spirit of Wisdom
And the way, the Truth
And the life embraces her
With love
In the living moment.

Then
She climbs the mountain
Of being and time
With the desire to experience
Full redemption
Of time and times and a half.

It is
By a leap of faith
That she feels
The presence of the angels
Of heaven

Those unidentified
Flying objects that define
The mystery of life.

Then
The dawn of faith
Fills the children of promise
With blessed assurance
As the scarlet rose
Travels into the heart
Of what matters.

So
Annabel Lee serves
The Unknown God
With devoted passion.

*

As she approached
Shadows of thought
A chill stilled her breath.

There was
An emptiness to the moment
As brain waves caved
Her mind into brittle shards
Of thought.

In the darkness
Of now moments
She followed brain waves
Through a portal
To a life of dry bones.

Then
Her life fell into a void.

Suddenly
The flesh of despair
Took her substance
And shook her
To her roots.

It was
The workings of dark magic
That pulled the strings
Attached to her mind
Triggering the sweat
Of desperation.

Searching for hope
She gathered her wits.

Then
She thought of the light
Of a one-dimensional reality
As she saw the whole body

Of Truth in the way
The Truth and the life.

Awakening from her moment
Of terror
She closed the lid of Pandora's box.

*

Although the dawn
Carried Truth
From The Spirit of Wisdom
The world closed its heart
To the freedom of the way
The Truth and the life.

Although a testament
To the dance
Of being toward Truth
Poured pure music in the air
The world could not breathe
The breath of freedom.

So
The brain waves
Of being and nothingness
Pyramided death onto life
And times distanced
The moment
From the here and now.

There was
Dark magic on the horizon
As the demigods raised
The flag of infamy.

Then
Lady Liberty connected
To the angels of heaven
And the unidentified
Flying objects struck
The fallen angels
With Truth and justice.

As the scarlet rose
Declared freedom for all
The puppet masters crashed
Into a sea of madness.

Although the greed of a few
Had sold the world into bondage
The children of promise
Were prepared for battle
In the war of principalities.

From the mountains
Of the always already there
Brain waves disarmed
The fallen angels
And the world turned
To The Unknown God

The foundation of Truth
And justice.

*

It was
The call to freedom
That reverberated
Within the hearts
Of the children
Of promise.

*

Searching for Truth and justice
Mind rode the rhythm
Of the universe
Into the far reaches
Of time and space.

Connecting to the angels
Of heaven, being toward Truth
Traveled into the frontier
Of endless possibility
As the unidentified
Flying objects liberated
Thought from all constraints.

There is
An opening of wonder
And splendor in the heart
Of blessed assurance

That transcends
The here and now
And treasures
Of pure music fills
The moment with Truth
And justice.

So
Annabel Lee ventured
Into horizons
Of endless possibility
Willing her way
Through the freedom
Of thought.

Then
Mind finds the scarlet rose
While bathing in the light
Of the always already there.

As her trance
Carried her into the dawn
Of what matters
Annabel Lee emerged
From the traffic
Of the dull round
To follow the dance
Of the scarlet rose.

Then
She trumpeted the work
Of The Spirit of Wisdom
As the UFO's pyramided
Life, liberty and the pursuit
Of happiness across
The here and now.

*

So
It was that the children
Of promise had not yet
Begun to fight
As Lady Liberty armed
Herself with weapons
Of Truth and justice.

So
The unidentified
Flying objects sided
With life, liberty
And the pursuit of happiness
As Annabel Lee throttled
Kindred spirits
Into the front lines
Of defense.

It was
With the power

Of the here and now
Aligned with angels of heaven
That took the fight
Against fallen angels.

So
The UFO's would center
Brain waves
Against the despots
Causing them to fester
With liver cancer.

One by one
The demigods would be
Stricken
As Lady Liberty flexed
The muscle of freedom.

So
The children of promise
Would discharge a weapon
Against the leaders of tyranny
While the people of the world
Would be unharmed.

Although the despots seek
Enslavement of the world
The Unknown God
Is in control
With the power

Of The Spirit of Wisdom
Through the way
The Truth and the life.

*

From a wilderness of dreams
The crystal crow drew
The energy of time and space
As being toward Truth
Yearned to serve Lady Liberty.

Within the bastions
Of heavenly bodies
He gathered focus
Upon the tyrants
Of the world
Infusing them with cancer
One by one.

It was
A top secret development
That the children
Of promise held
As The crystal crow leaned
Upon the understanding
Of The Spirit of Wisdom.

It was
His faith in the way

The Truth and the life
That aligned him
To the UFO's
As the power mongers
Squirmed with fear.

So
Annabel Lee announced
The development
Of a breakthrough
In technology equipping
The land of the free
And the brave
With the dynamics
Of unidentified
Flying objects.

In time and times
And a half
This new weapon
Would be dispatched.

So
The targets
Of this brain wave
Technology
Were warned to stand down.

Then
The crystal crow turned

To worship at the altar
Of The Unknown God.

*

Drawing from the deep touch
Of trance, the artist
Pictured the breath of tyrants
Inhaling the seeds of cancer
As their time was running out.

There was
An incision of immanent death
Upon the faces of demigods
As the unidentified
Flying objects charged time
And times and a half
With the attack upon them.

So
The fallen angels would be
Sent to the second death
In a lake of fire.

Then
The UFO's connected
The rhythm of the universe
To the pulse of the tyrants
Corrupting their hearts.

All the artist wanted
Was to live and let live
And for the world
To live in peace
But the power mongers
Would not leave
Their greed for control.

Although he warned
The puppet masters
To cease and desist
They did not listen
Because they did not
Believe in the power
Of The Unknown God.

Then
The drums of eternity
Echoed in their minds
Warning them to turn
From their evil ways.

So
A trumpet sounded.

*

So
The artist felt thoughts
In a wilderness of dreams

As thunder from the beyond
Crashed upon his mind.

Then
An awakening to being
Toward Truth took
Him into the mystery of life
As the rhythm
Of the universe filled him
With The Spirit of Wisdom.

Although the despots
Tried to cancel spirituality
The scarlet rose gathered
The children of promise
Into an arsenal of brain waves
Focused with the energy
Of the encompassing.

It is
That freedom of spirituality
Allows Truth and justice
To prevail.

It is
That the unknown
Allows a leap of faith
Into what matters
Since hidden meaning

Writes curiosity
Into the heart.

To probe endless possibility
Allows the inner eye
To prosper
As the scarlet rose
Carries mind into the way
The Truth and the life.

So
The children of promise unite
With the angels of heaven
As Lady Liberty secures
The place of freedom
With pure music.

*

Driven by the passion
For Truth and justice
She meditated
Upon The Spirit of Wisdom
While an old man
Took to the rhythm
Of the universe.

It was
A leap of faith
That grew being toward Truth

From the earth
Of being and nothingness
As the old man launched
A multitude of brain waves
Across time and space
That registered
In the inner eye
Of corrupt hearts.

So
Humbled before the glory
Of The Unknown God
The children of promise
United with the way
The Truth and the life
As the old man felt
The passion of Lady Liberty
For Truth and justice.

Then
Times and a half passed.

It was
That the greed
Of the power mongers
Came to a point
Of no return
And the destiny
Of the blue planet
Would burn life alive.

So
This was the picture
That the artist painted
As the madness
Of the world capsized
Into annihilation.

So
She is his touchstone
To the unknown.

*

As she dances
Pure music in the air
Trumpets sound
And mind crawls
Into the center
Of the mystery of life.

Returning from the edge
Of endless possibility
Her thoughts register
The image of raw power
As her inner eye
Follows the rhythm
Of the universe
To what matters.

Standing in the wilds
She orchestrates memories
Of times and a half
Into the dawn
Of visions beyond thought.

Then
her dance liberates
being toward Truth
From the prison
Holding his mind
Captive
As she feels her way
Into the living moment
With his inner eye.

Then
The artist follows her
To the dark side
Of the moon.

Although they become
Twin beams
Headed to the glory
Of The Unknown God
There are brain waves
From fallen angels
Interfering with their passage.

To fight their way
Through oppression
The artist pictures
The dance of Lady Liberty
Over the threat
Of a broken mind.

So
The tyrants
No longer have vital signs.

*

As he dances
Pure music in the air
Trumpets sound
And mind crawls
Into the center
Of the mystery of life.

Returning from the edge
Of endless possibility
Her thoughts register
The image of raw power
As her inner eye
Follows the rhythm
Of the universe
To his muscle of passion.

Standing in the wilds
Of imagination
She orchestrates
Time and times
And a half
Into the dawn
Of visions
Beyond thought.

Then
His dance liberates
Being toward Truth
From the constraints
Of an attack
Upon his mind
As she feels her way
Into the living moment
With her inner eye.

Then
The artist follows her
To the dark side
Of the moon.

Although they become
Twin beams
Headed to the light
Of a one dimensional reality
There are brain waves
From fallen angels

Interfering with their
Passage.

To battle their way
Through the madness
Of being and time
The scarlet rose pictures
The dance of pure music
Over the threat
Of a broken mind.

So
The oppressors
have no vital signs
Any more.

*

As mind drifts
Through clouds
Of hidden meaning
Being toward Truth
Rises from the darkness
Of being and time
And the scarlet rose
Dances the deep touch
Into the living moment.

It was
Time to hunt fallen angels.

Through a looking glass
The scarlet rose
Configured a lure
To fish out the corrupt.

So
There was a challenge
To the scarlet rose.

Plunging into trance
She emits brain waves
Across time and space
With the power
Of Truth and justice.

Then
She excavates the meat
Of being and nothingness
With her succulent beauty.

Then
With precision
She triggers brain waves
Across time and space
To strike a particular despot.

So
The scarlet rose teaches
The deep touch as a weapon

Liberating the oppressed
With a passionate

*

Surrounded by sirens
Of death and destruction
Lady Liberty conceives herself
Beyond the corrupt rhetoric
Of living infamy.

There is
the sound of alarm
across horizons of time
as the scarlet rose defends
life, liberty and the pursuit
of happiness
as Lady Liberty faces
the doctrine of dread.

In the heart
Of the land from sea
To shining sea
A song of freedom
Fills the living moment
As Truth goes
Marching on.

Then
Echoes of wagaloo
Occupy time and space.

Then
The thunder of what matters
Opens the way, the Truth
And the life
With the dance of forevermore
And the children of promise
March into battle
To return Lady Liberty
To the land of milk
And honey.

Then
The fallen angels crumble
With a legacy
Of abominations
As The Spirit of Wisdom
Unites the children
Of promise.

So
The scarlet rose restores
Truth and justice
To the rightful place
As the corner stone
Of living life

Then
The Unknown God smiles.

*

So
It is unidentified
Flying objects
That belong to the unknown
As the world ignores
The Truth.

So
UFO's are
The materialization
Of brain waves
Feeding upon
The deep touch
Of The Spirit of Wisdom.

As the trumpet sounds
Truth centers the reality
Of endless possibility
And the scarlet rose
Climbs into hidden meaning
With the light
Of a one dimensional
Reality.

So
Abandoned by the world
An old man staggers
Into the grave.

He is the witness
Of the way, the Truth
And the life
As the world grinds
His mind into dust.

It is
His faith
In The Unknown God
Through the workings
Of the way, the Truth
And the life
That comforts him
As the here and now
Defines being and nothingness
And his mind reaches
The other side
Of the beyond.

Reading the spaces
Of hidden meaning
He turns to the scarlet rose
And she eases his pain.

How
Deep the wounds
Festering a being toward Truth
Bur there is
The dream of the scarlet rose.

*

Dancing through time and space
The scarlet rose liberates
The moment from captivity
As the artist traces
Her elegance in his mind.

Flowing with the rhythm
Of the universe
She releases brain waves
Through the always
Already there that sing
The splendor of pure music
Into the skull of humanity.

She is love and she is beauty.

So
The scarlet rose
Multiplies life
In the living moment
As the treasures
Of the beyond deposit
The deep touch of freedom
And she weaponizes brain waves
To reform the corrupt.

She is Truth and she is justice
And she is dangerous.

As she focuses
Her energy on the demigod
The heart of the target
Bursts into bloody meat.

For those who violate
The integrity of being
Toward Truth
There is no escape
From judgement.

As a warrior of freedom
She battles against the corrupt
With precision and quickly
Disables their greed.

So
The artist pictures her
As Lady Liberty
His trophy wife
In the here and now.

So
Her substance is lethal
To those who violate
Her dance
Of freedom across
The here and now.

*

So
The circle forms
The mission of the way
The Truth and the life
As the corrupt cringe
In their castles
Of ashes.

So
Lady Liberty charges
Into battle
As a freedom warrior
And the artist
Testifies to the presence
Of The Spirit of Wisdom.

It is
That from the living moment
Ideas appear
On the horizon and they liberate
The children of promise
From those bent on enslaving them.

The desire for freedom
Is the force
That cannot be constrained
As the warriors of Truth
Carry five smooth stones.

So
The connection to the angels
Of heaven eases
The authentic article
Into being toward Truth
While the puppet masters
Are confounded by the UFO's
A mystery of life.

Covered by the living moment
The artist emanates Truth and justice
Into the heart of the world
As the war of principalities
Rages over the here and now.

Then
He awakens life, liberty
And the pursuit of happiness
To a bold new world.

*

Entering endless possibility
Searching through the unknown
Deciphering hidden meaning
The artist proceeds
In meditation
As time and space
Dissolve in the in inevitable.

It is
In the living moment
When the here and now
Explodes into pure music
That he rides
The rhythm of the universe.

As mind drinks in
What matters
The mystery of life
Dances across thoughts
And the vision
Of the always already there
Opens the beyond
To the experiential.

Then
The artist connects
To The Spirit of Wisdom.

Then
The scarlet rose allows him
To experience life, liberty
And the pursuit of happiness
And freedom flows
Into the inner eye
Of being toward Truth.

Connecting to the way
The Truth and the life

The artist testifies
To the glory of the way
The Truth and the life
As the scarlet rose
Opens his heart
To Lady Liberty.

Then
The vision of the house
Of many mansions
Welcomes them
To the presence
Of The Unknown God.

*

As she fought her way back
From the dark side
The hollow of her heart
Cried out for deliverance.

Facing the arsenal
Of the corrupt
She cruised into silence
From shadows
Of being and nothingness.

Then
Her brain waves
Triggered the collapse

Of their castles
As they turned
Into heaps of ashes.

As the will
Of the scarlet rose
Strengthened, the angels
Of heaven navigated
Through a gauntlet
In time and space.

So
To control the seas
Meant the control of commerce
As the puppet masters
Prepared for a sea war
With their intent
To rule the world.

So
It was the scarlet rose
Annabel Lee and Lady Liberty
That carried light
Into the dark side
As the corrupt stirred
Destruction into the wind
While the UFO's strengthened
The will of the children
Of promise.

It was
That the power of freedom
Fed upon The Spirit
Of Wisdom as a greater sense
Diffused the unleashing
Of a nuclear war.

So
The corrupt backed down.

*

It was
The morning before the end
When she looked death
In the eye and laughed
At its nakedness.

There was
Truth in the wind
As time wound down
And the seed of destruction
Was sewn into mind.

Holding onto life
She gathered the breath
Of another day
And marched off to war.

There were bombs
Bursting in the air
As the authentic article
Kissed her cheek.

Then
She assumed herself
Into a two-dimensional
Reality.

Consuming the living moment
She spotted an unidentified
Flying object
As an angel of heaven
Filled her heart
With pure music.

There was
A slight of hand
That touched her brain
As dark magic tried
To corrupt her.

Then
A rant of terror captured
The thoughts of the artist.

Then
He pictured

The death of all
And everything.

Deconstructing
The here and now
A fallen angel
Manipulated what was
There, but life, liberty
And the pursuit
Of happiness lived on.

Then
The scarlet rose experienced
The Spirit of Wisdom.

*

Leaving a time warp
When the here and now dissolves
In endless possibility
The artist gathers
The bones of the actual
To reconstruct the veritable
As the scarlet rose
Allows him visions
Of the mystery of life.

In the looking glass
Of what matters
The mystery of life

Had taken him
Into the rubric of nonbeing
Where he felt
The power of the unknown.

It was
An adventure
Into the intelligence
Behind the UFO's.

It was
The allowing
Of the brain waves
From deep space
That carried him
Into the life
Of the scarlet rose.

It was
A dance with the angels
Of heaven.

Drawing upon the substance
Of being toward Truth
The artist reclaimed
His life in actuality.

So
The pure music

Of the always already there
Staggered his mind.

So
The mystery of life
Had reached
Into his substance.

*

Although the brain waves
Of infamy permeated
The here and now
Lady Liberty seizes
The living moment
To tap into pure music
And the power
Of blessed assurance triumphs
Over the existential moment.

There is
Thunder in the blood
Of the children of promise
That eclipses deconstruction
And the scarlet rose launches
Freedom into the hearts
Of the oppressed
As the puppet masters
Are thrown into the abyss.

So
The struggle continues.

It is
That The Spirit of Wisdom
Wills Truth and justice
Over being and nothingness
As the angels of heaven
Gather the forces
Of the children of promise.

Then
The dark magic
Of the demigods dissolves
In a one-dimensional reality
As their brain waves
Are cast into dry places.

So
The artist pictures
Life, liberty and the pursuit
Of happiness
As Annabel Lee poses
The peace beyond understanding.

So
Lady Liberty celebrates
The glory
Of The Unknown God.

*

When the trumpet sounded
The scarlet rose marched
Into battle
That should have struck
Fear into the heart
Of the oppressors
For they should have known
That their time had come.

It was
No myth or fabrication
That she led the unidentified
Flying objects
Into the strong hold
Of the corrupt.

It was
The brain waves of the UFO's
That wielded the power
Of The Unknown God.

So the elements of tyranny
Would be expunged.

Through their greed for power
They had blocked out
Their destiny in a lake of fire

Because they chose to think
That God is dead.

They had come to think
That the second death
Was a fairy tale
To teach children obedience.

It is
That the cause
Of Lady Liberty
Is the link
To the always already there
As Truth and justice
Determined the destiny
Of the puppet masters
And the celestial clocks
Struck the hour of their doom.

So
The children of promise
Followed The Spirit of Wisdom
As warriors
Of the way, the Truth
And the life.

So
All is quiet
On the eastern front.

SECTION 3

LIVING IN THE NATURAL WORLD

Indwelling
Before the beginning
Of time and space
The Spirit of Wisdom
Issues the rhythm
Of the universe, carrying
The mystery of life
Through pure music.

It is
The song of eternity
Dressing being toward Truth
In the garments of the always
Already there
As the drums of eternity
Bring life
Into the living moment.

Then
The legends of time past
Are conceived
Upon Precambrian rocks
And rivers of thought
Document a history
Of time and times
And a half.

Suddenly
An artist walks
Out of being and nothingness

To envision history
As a living thing.

So
It is an awakening
To the way, the Truth
And the life
With thoughts projecting
The celestial clocks
As witnesses to what matters.

Then
The artist crawls
Into the here and now
Recording visions
Of life, liberty and the pursuit
Of happiness.

Then
The crystal crow
Speaks the language
Of the authentic article
in the tongue
Of The Unknown God.

*

In the valley of dry bones
The crystal crow emerges
As a freedom fighter

To decipher hidden meaning
For the children of promise
As the full face of the moon
Defines the life of time.

Out of the shadows
Of the unknown
Endless possibility kisses
Being toward Truth
While the language
Of the unidentified
Flying objects allow
The rise of pure music.

Then
The crystal crow dances
In the sky
Welcomed to the dawn
Of being toward Truth.

There is
A certain strength
In his heart that follows
The rhythm of the universe
As the celestial clocks
Strike the hour
With an existential moment.

Although the crystal crow
Speaks the language

Of The Spirit of Wisdom
The world is swallowed up
By the greed for power
While in the valley of dry
bones Truth comes alive.

So
He listens to the way
The Truth and the life
As the moon lights
A message of hope.

So
The children of promise
Are in the world
But not of the world.

*

Connecting
To the deep touch
the crystal crow
Launched a probe
Into the other side
Of deep space, the source
Of the rhythm of the universe.

There was
A message written
In the sky

Leading Lady Liberty
And the children
Of promise into battle.

To defend life, liberty
And the pursuit of happiness
Is their mission.

So
The crystal crow
Had gathered the intelligence
Leading the will for Truth.

There was
No turning back
Because Truth and justice
Must be served.

So
The scarlet rose
Had partnered with crystal crow
To infiltrate the ranks
Of the axis powers.

Danger bled
Across time and space.

So
Through the invasion
From the southern border

Nuclear suitcases were
Smuggled in.

So
The crystal crow
And the scarlet rose
Tracked them by reading
Their brain waves
Accessed by the deep touch
Through the rhythm
Of the universe.

*

Overcome
With somnambulism
The crystal crow lived
In his dreams.

It is
That he had attached
To the scarlet rose
Because he is her favorite.

So
She took him
Into her folds
Through brain waves
And he felt the rise
Of the authentic article

Move his substance
With her heart.

Although her deep touch
Brought him wonders
Of sensation
She shared her duty
In his dreams.

They trumpeted
The crystal crow
Into being toward Truth
Equipping him
With the ability to decipher
The hidden meaning
Of oppressors.

So
She shared him
With the unidentified
Flying objects
Setting a solid foundation
For life, liberty
And the pursuit of happiness.

As a vertical column
Of time nourished him
With visions of the unknown
The scarlet rose invited
His nakedness into her mind.

So
The crystal crow
Was enabled to decipher
The brain waves
Of tyrant regimes.

*

Then
Mind intercepts a communique
Of brain waves fastened
To the darkness
And the crystal crow
Catches it from the wind.

It is
About the invasion
At the southern border
Infecting the stars and stripes
With dark magic.

So
It all was about a plot
To rape Lady Liberty
And hold her captive
Depriving her of freedom.

There is
A quiet majesty
In her look

That transcends
The here and now.
There is
Grace in her step
As she dances
With the majesty of life
In her song of pure music.

So
The scarlet rose takes
To deep space
Moving the calculus
Of the celestial clocks
To a time of power and strength
As the crystal crow launches
Fire into the heart
Of the oppressors.

So
It is war.

So
Annabel Lee surrounds
The muscle of the tyrants
With the passion pf freedom
As the substance
Of the crystal crow
Saturates the moment
With life, liberty

And the pursuit
Of happiness.

*

Drinking in his fountain
Of youth, she awakens
To his dream of the dance
Of being toward Truth
Between here and there
Enlightening the moment
To the mystery of life.

There is the Truth
Beyond understanding
That exacerbates
The existential threat
As the scarlet rose
Spreads her vision
Far into the unknown.

It is
That he serves Lady Liberty
With all chips in
As the gamble for freedom
Is a safe bet.

Devoted to life, liberty
And the pursuit of happiness
The crystal crow

Consummates his love
On the battlefield.

It is
That he penetrates
The stronghold
Of the oppressors
Transforming their endeavors
Into much ado about nothing.

Denied of a voice
The demigods retreat
Into the eternal lake
Of fire, as the children
Of promise triumph
Over their doublespeak.

Then
The language
Of Truth and justice
Penetrates all
Of the three-dimensional
Reality
As the crystal crow
Serves freedom
With fervent passion.

*

Back in the garden
Of tables and chairs
She pointed to the invasion
Of time and space
As the death of thought.

Although deconstructionists
Tried to cancel the way
The Truth and the life
From the living moment
The will of The Unknown God
Fortified the children
Of promise to stand strong.

Then
She attached herself
To the rhythm
Of the universe
And her dance
Of freedom mesmerized
The existential threat.

It was
That the reset
Of the pandemic
Caused chaos to rule
As the puppet masters
Canceled Truth and justice.

So
She had bonded
With the crystal crow
And the life of their warriors
Took the world into freedom.

So
The demigods had no chance
Of escaping from the thunder
Of the mystery of life, as their will
To power marked their demise.

*

Reading between the lines
Of hidden meaning
Unveils the brainwaves
Of the oppressors
As the crystal crow
Advances into the mystery of life.

After receiving the deep touch
He climbs out of himself
To face the existential threat.

It is
The madness
Of being and time
That threatens
The living moment

When the authentic article
Pyramids Truth and justice
Into the heart
Of the crystal crow.

So
His muscle is engaged
As the scarlet rose
Pulls his substance
Into being toward Truth.

As they gather
The children of promise
To launch the power
Of pure music
The demigods creep
Into their destruction.

So
The fallen angels had plotted
To rule the world
With their language
Of doublespeak.

There is
No Truth in them
As they stumble
Into their end.

Then
A song discards them
Into the silent flames
Of their grave.

*

Pyramiding through
Time and space
The crystal crow
Visits the wind
As he probes
Brain waves.

Following the drift
Of hidden meaning he feels
The deep touch
Uncovering the lair
Of a puppet master.

It is
That the crystal crow
Taps into the heart
Of tyrants
Launching a defensive
Attack.

As the seed of conflict
Grows into the brain
Of the oppressors

The celestial clocks strike
The hour with condemnation.

There is no escape.

Then
The crystal crow launches
An abyss into the targets.

Time and times and a half
With a crippling effect.

Although the puppet masters
Are impaired
They experience a reckoning
To their condemnation.
Beaten by their own folly
They withdraw their troops
And the land rejoices
In the rebirth of freedom.

*

There is a song weaving kindness
In the air
As the world
Cries out in the darkness.

It is
A song pitched

With the rhythm
Of the universe
That lifts the down-trodden
As the living moment
Drinks in pure music.

How
Annabel Lee swoons
Before the melody
That releases joy
To the world
As the rebirth
Of freedom delivers
Life, liberty and the pursuit
Of happiness.

So
She dances through time
And times and a half
With the symmetry
Of being toward Truth
And the darkness
Of the moment
Turns to the splendor
Of dawn.

As the tyrants
Of the age takes refuge
In the lake of fire
The children of promise

Hear the message
Of the crystal crow.

His bond
To Annabel Lee
Serves a dream
Of waggaloo
Across the three-dimensional
Reality.

So
Their legacy endures
Onto forevermore.

*

Undercover with the deep touch
The crystal crow ferrets his way
To an alternate reality
Where being and time
Conjures hell fire.

To bring an end
To tyrants
And their madness
He follows the rhythm
Of the universe
To the heart
Of the oppressors.

Following the brainwaves b
Of Annabel Lee the silence
Of a moment between
The real and the not real.

It is
That he pumps through
A two-dimensional
Reality onto an explosion
As the demigods
Disintegrate in their own
Greed for power.

Then
Annabel Lee focuses
A weaponized brain wave
Onto the mind of the despots.

So
It is another cold war.

It is
Good that the unidentified
Flying objects are with her.

As the angels of heaven
Attend to the crystal crow
Behind the scenes
Annabel Lee and the children
Of promise establish life

Liberty and the pursuit
Of happiness in the place
Of the despots.

*

Cradled in the hands
Of the scarlet rose
The crystal crow sees
The rhythm of the universe
Carry love across the here
And now.

He is a man on duty
Following her tune
And trumpeting pure music
With his being toward Truth.

Composing himself into time
And space
He feels the mystery of life
Come into visions
Of the always already there
As they bring Truth and justice
Into a world of chaos.

Then he marches into battle.

It is
A passion for life

Liberty and the pursuit
Of happiness that he
Forms the substance of love
Proving her grip
On his wants and needs.

So
The scarlet rose
Serves the land
Of the free and brave
While Annabel Lee
Allows him to see
What matters.

Together they detect
The trucking
Of a nuclear suitcase
With the invasion
From the southern border.

So
His inner eye tracks
Pending doom
And the children of promise
Snuff it out.

*

In tender moments
Of meditation

The crystal crow feels
His way into pure music
As the celestial clocks
Strike the hour
To transcend beyond
The madness of the world.

There is
A passage of time
When mind hunkers down
As the heart
Of being and nothingness
Follows the rhythm
Of the universe
Onto forevermore.

Then
He sees the work
Of The Spirit of Wisdom.

Then
The drums of eternity
Pound life into an awakening
Of being toward Truth
And the scarlet rose breathes
The way, the Truth
And the life into orbits
Of what matters.

It is
That the message is blurred
By the language of demigods
As Truth bleeds into the abyss.

Then
The mystery of life
Resurrects the way
The Truth and the life
As the crystal crow feeds
The scarlet rose
With eternal light.

So
Their inner eye
Beholds the always
Already there
Of The Unknown God.

*

Transitioning into a new life
The crystal crow imagines
A world of Truth and justice
As the dull round explodes
With anarchy.

Waiting for the scarlet rose
He fashioned what matters
In accordance

With The Unknown God
As the blood of a world
Soured in the soil
Of the will to power.

It was
The trumpeting
Of the children of promise
That brought the unidentified
Flying objects from the other
Side of the sky
As the neanderthals
Overturned the tyranny
Of the homo sapiens.

Drinking in
The secrets of the universe
The crystal crow loo0ked
To life, liberty and the pursuit
Of happiness
To return to the neanderthals
As he cut the wires
Of the puppet masters.

Then
Lady Liberty formed
A more perfect union
With roots
To the way, the Truth
And the life

As the children of promise
Prospered in the dawn
Of deliverance.

Listening to the pure music
Of The Spirit Wisdom
They cultivated a garden
Of tables and chairs
Where the UFO's brought
Living water to the thirsty.

*

In a wilderness
Of time and space
The crystal crow designs
The here and now
As the scarlet rose travels
Through his mind.

There is
Ab ruckus in the moment
As the world spins
Wildly out of control
And the gravity
Of being and time
Weighs through the flesh
Of being toward Truth.

To turn
To the way, the Truth
And the life
Liberates thought
From the prison
Enforced by puppet
Masters, the thought police.

Then
Freedom escapes
With The Spirit of Wisdom
Onto the free and brave
And pure music mirrors
Times and a half
Across the ages.

How
The rhythm
Of the universe delivers
Life, liberty and the pursuit
Of happiness
As the answer to death
Is the living moment.

Then
The crystal crow parades
Freedom into the heart
Of what matters
And trumpets salute
The life of Lady Liberty.

Then
The scarlet rose dances
In the presence
Of The Unknown God.

*

It must have been
A dream
That carried him
Into the battle
For all the chips
As trumpets drew swords
And bombs burst
In the air.

There was
Power in the way
The Truth and the life
That formed peace
Beyond understanding
As mind rejected
thought control
as a reckoning
of imagination
but it was true
that the crystal crow
could intercept
brain waves.

It must have been
That dark magic
Took a pound of flesh
As deliverance
From the demigods.

Then
A vision of pure music
Endorsed individual freedom
As the foundation
Of being toward Truth
And the crystal crow's focus
Turned to the revolution
To a dynamic reset.

It was
The preservation of Lady Liberty
That took hold of him.

Although
The work of fallen angels welled up
From the will to power
Lady Liberty called upon
The children of promise
To fight the good fight.

So
Blood filled the seas
Onto forevermore.

*

SECTION 4

TANGLED IN NOTHINGNESS

Picking up
Where he left off
His tour of duty
Brought tears
In the eyes
Of his son
As time and space
Opened
To an endless journey.

It was
The crystal crow
Advancing across
The rice paddy
As lead blistered
Through times and a half.

So
What is death
When it is
All or nothingness.

So
There are worse things
Than being
A prisoner of war.

Feeling his way
Into a great escape
He lived on bugs and mud

Following the footsteps
Of being toward Truth.

So

Lost in a rice paddy
He laid low
As water turned
Blood red from all the blood.

So

They called him
The unknown soldier
Just another GI
Who met his maker
Far too early
For a life of promise.

Weeds come and go
But the scarlet rose
Lives on
In the heart
Of the free and brave.

So

Is the cost of freedom.

*

It was
At the edge

Of time and space
That the crystal crow
Assessed the gravity
Of an existential threat.

He looked into the abyss
And he looked
To The Spirit of Wisdom
Finding his vision
Stretching far beyond
The here and now.

Then
The scarlet rose
Danced
Across his mind
As thoughts of her fed
His substance
With what matters
And the crystal crow
Pictured the plot
Against the order of things.

It was
The presence
Of the way, the Truth
And the life
That purposed him
To intercept their brain waves

As they announced revolution
From shadows of actuality.

So
A horizon of secrets
Whispered to his mind
With the poison
Of upheaval and assassination.

Behind what was there
He intercepted the brain waves
Of a plot by those greedy
For power
Deciphering the intrigue
Of the despots
As the triumph
Of light over dark magic
Healed the wounds
Cast by their will to power.

So
It was to stand strong
With faith
In The Unknown God
That allowed freedom
To endure in the land
Of milk and honey.

*

Riding on the rhythm
Of the universe
The crystal crow advances
Into the unknown
Intercepting the brain waves
Of secret dealings.

There is
An echo of Truth
In the wind
As times and a half
Pass into darkness.

Dwelling among the children
Of promise, he reaches
Through meditation
To the harbors of thought
And he basks in the light
Of the way, the Truth
And the life
As a parabola of time
Infuses the living moment
With visions
Of what matters.

Then
The blood of being toward Truth
Flows as the cost of freedom
And the crystal crow erects a wall
Of defenses.

Under attack
The children of promise
Follow him
With the authentic
Article
Onto the battlefield
Of the here and now
As their faith
In The Unknown God
Carries them
Onto the narrow path
Of Truth and justice.

Although the despots
Starve a world of Truth
The crystal crow rises
With the power
Of the deep touch
Liberating mind
From the thought police.

*

So
Basking in the light
Of a one-dimensional
Reality
With trumpets sounding
The moment outside of time
The artist launched

His mind beyond thought
And into the always
Already there.

It was
That his being toward Truth
Had sought what matters
And what is
The substance behind
What is there.

He wanted to paint
The mystery of life
And to stretch his mind
Across the unknown.

It was
A matter of first principles
That seemed
To have an obstruction
Surrounding its stand.

So
He turned
To the way, the Truth
And the life
To gain access
To an understanding.

Following his faith
He sought
The Spirit of Wisdom
To take him
Beyond the immediate.

Certainly
He thought there must be
More than his life
As the sun set
On an understanding
Of the dull round.

Then
He entered the always
Already there.

Then
He felt the rise
Of his being toward Truth
In the presence
Of The Unknown God.

Then
Looking from the beyond
He had seen a nuclear
Suitcase coming across
The southern border.

So
How many were there?

*

Tapping into the deep touch
The artist receives a vision
From the other side
Of time and space.

It is
A fabrication of the actual
That fills the air
With clouds of deception
Passing half truths
As the authentic article.

There is the angst
Of this existential threat
Dangling in the wind.

Then
The artist translates
The brain waves
Of this evil into an image.

It is
The cry of what matters
As the first principles
Are founded upon a given.

So
Assumptions fade
Into the mask
Of a leap of faith
As theory is based
Upon a best guess.

Then
The artist imagines
The face of Truth
And she is love
Grounded in the peace
Beyond understanding.

*

So
They spit on our flag
And chairman crystal crow
Spoke hell fire across the globe.

It was
All or nothing
Playing for all the chips
The mother load
As the war room assembled
To teach the demigods
Who was in charge.

It was
A matter of freedom
And defending Lady Liberty.

It was
A matter of life, liberty
And the pursuit of happiness
That was at stake.

So
We had not yet
Begun to fight.

On the home front
It was law and order
For all
With no exceptions
And the puppet masters
Shook in their high heals.

It was
Putting to death
The cancel culture
And re-establishing
The children of promise
As free spirits.

It was
Living the dream
For one and all

In the land
Of opportunity.

*

Although Lady Liberty
Is surrounded
By fallen angels
A sanctuary city
Is established as a course
Of events.

So
It was destiny
Unfolding that turned
A grievous tragedy
Into a vibrant hope
For women and children
As a truce ended
Twenty years of war.

It was
A city that became
A jewel of commerce
Opening freedom
For a multitude.

How
Opportunity occurred

To turn a tragic evil
Into a veritable good.

It was
A wild and reckless dream
That covered the moment
Asa the puppet masters
Trembled before the face
Of The Unknown God.

As time wore
A crown of glory
It came to pass
That the world
Opened its eyes
To life, liberty
And the pursuit
Of happiness.

As the revolution
Of time and times
And a half eased
The peace beyond understanding
Into the heart of darkness
Truth and justice lit
The way for Neanderthals
To grab the gold ring.

*

Awakening to the actual
The artist rose
From the depths
Of time and space
Foreseeing the thunder
Of freedom pounding
Pure music into the living
Moment.

Although chaos
Was at the front door
It was good to be alive
In the land
Of the free and brave.

Configuring first principles
From the base
Of the way
The Truth and the life
He looked to the scarlet rose
For an ally against
The existential threat
Of the puppet masters.

It was
That mind control
Through hijacking brain waves
Was the enemy.

So
The artist rode
The rhythm of the universe
To a fully function
Self-actualizing individual.

So
He lived in his life
Through liberty
And pursuing happiness
Among first principles
While visions stirred
From the recesses
Of what matters.

As the scarlet rose
Took his heart
To the altar
Eternity opened the doorway
To The Spirit of Wisdom.

So
After long imprisonment
In dark magic
The artist was free
To share the secrets
Embedded
In the mystery of life.

*

It was
From the unidentified
Flying objects
That reached into his substance
Stirring visions
Of the other side
Of time and space
As the artist pyramided
Into being and nothingness.

As the chemistry
Of the mystery of life
Released him to serve
Life, liberty and the pursuit
Of happiness
He felt the deep touch
Of the scarlet rose.

Then
The struggle
Of being toward Truth
Rose in sweat
As the scarlet rose
Saluted his attention.

Bringing the dance
Of muscle and blood
The artist engineered
Passage onto a parabola
Of time.

Then
The scarlet rose embraced
His dignity
And the living moment
Painted an existential
Threat across his mind.

It was
That the brain waves
Of the despots
Were intercepted
By the deep touch
Of the UFO's
As the scarlet rose engaged
Flesh of the artist.

So
The demigods burned
In their own folly.

*

Suddenly
Wild orbs of an alien substance
Broke across the horizon
As pure music poured
Into the living moment
And the drums of eternity
Pounded the always already there
Into organic thoughts.

Then
The crystal crow launched
Into the center
Of a parabola of time
As the lights of forevermore
Guided his journey
Into the unknown.

There was
The mystery of life
Weaving the way
The Truth and the life
Across his heart
As he felt the approach
Of The Spirit of Wisdom.

So
The image
Of being toward Truth
Proceeded into forevermore.

As the crystal crow
Opened his inner eye
To being band nothingness
Trumpets proclaimed
The death of dark magic.

Although it was engulfed
In neck breaking turmoil
The land of the children

Of promise marched
Into victory over the despots
As Lady Liberty prevailed.
And the scarlet rose
Kissed the land
Of the free and brave.

It is
Freedom that allows
Truth and justice to flourish
As the pure music
Of The Unknown God
Preserves and protects
The independence
Of each soul.

*

Across the horizon
Trumpets sounded life
Liberty and the pursuit
Of happiness
As the doctrine
Of the landscape.

It was
A time when kindred spirits
Cried out for Truth
And justice

And the leaders hid
Beneath shadows.

So
The so-called weeds
Blossomed
Into beauteous blooms
And their scent
Enriched the world
With power and might.

Stepping into the line
Of fire, the crystal crow
Shielded Lady Liberty
From harm.

To have the courage
To take a stand
And draw a line
In the sand
The kindred spirits rose
With the rising sun.

So
We have not yet
Begun to fight
Echoed across the world
As the land
Of the free and brave
Took a large stick

Pounding light
Into dark magic.

Then
The kindred spirits marched
Into combat
And the terrorists trembled.

So
The crystal crow led
The charge of freedom
Into the heart of the terrorists.

*

When a point
Of the mystery of life
Becomes an account
Of the actual
Time and space explode
Into understanding.

It is
That clever minds
Conjure dark magic
Out of the pain
Of others
As the fallen angels hide
In the debris
Of their devastation.

So
The cruel abuse
In childhood
Leaves wounds festering
For a life time.

Then
The crystal crow mounts
Destiny with enduring
Courage.

So
There are those
Totally corrupt
That inflict wounds
Festering for a life time
Until one day
The Truth wills out.

Then
It is time
To carry on
Fulfilling destiny
With the knowledge
Of the always already
There.

So
The crystal crow takes
To pure music

Liberating the soul
From all oppression
As the love for freedom
Speaks parables
In the wind.

*

As a fog engulfed the world
A purple haze filled
The hearts of time
And times and a half.

It was
A progression of heart speak
With power and strength
Until swamped by the abyss
And mud clogged the lungs
Of being and nothingness.

Stepping back
From the front lines
Lady Liberty gathered resolve
Focusing her will
On a winning strategy
With power and strength
And the kindred spirits
Those children of promise
Fortified being toward Truth
With determination.

No existential threat
Has a chance
Against the power and strength
Of the land of the free
And brave.

Then
Thunder roared in the blood
Of being toward Truth
As an anthem
Of pure music pyramided
Time and space
Into a crushing force.

So
The determination
Of Lady Liberty issued
An invincible force
And the barbarians buckled
Drinking their own blood.

So
It was a reckoning
To life, liberty
And the pursuit of happiness
That silenced the barbarians.

Then
The world saluted

The stars and stripes
With respect and thanks.

*

Approaching the other side
Of the sky
Where time and space
Dance with the passion
Of the moment
The crystal crow feels
His way into the unknown.

Looking for a connection
To the peace beyond
Understanding
He follows the rhythm
Of the universe to the start
Of being toward Truth
As pure music elevates
His mind to the persona
Of the scarlet rose.

As she dances with his heart
The mind spins to an orbit
Around being and nothingness
And visions of what matters
Seize the moment.

It is
The passage of thoughts
That she harnesses
As she rides his mind
Into the muscle
Of the mystery of life.

Then
They travel across the frontier
Of imagining
As the deep touch
Lifts them into song.

Then
The scarlet rose issues
The nectar of the everlasting
And the crystal crow
Speaks with the tongue
Of the always already there.

So
The other side of the sky
Releases an awesome wonder
That carries their brain waves
Into endless possibility.

Then, time stops.

*

As their brain waves
Pass through time and space
They unite with the rhythm
Of the universe
Liberated from the constraints
Of the dull round.

There is
A song in their heart
That transforms
The mystery of life
Into a way of Truth
As they embrace
The living moment
With passion.

Then
Endless possibility opens
To the threshold
Of the beyond
As they form pure music
Through the magic
Of imagination.

So
The scarlet rose dances
Into the far reaches
Of his mind
As the crystal crow
Pyramids into what matters.

Although the world
Spins wildly into chaos
They ease into the comfort
Of each other's arms.

Basking in the warmth
Of the deep touch
Their brainwaves
Spirit being toward Truth
Into forevermore.

Then
They guide their now
Into the always already there
As the drums of eternity
Echo Truth throughout
Time and times and a half.

So
Dreams of kisses surround
Their time with ecstasy.

So
Their brainwaves allow them
To endure the threat
Of being and time.

Then
The scarlet rose rides
The deep touch

Into the dreams
Of the crystal crow
As their brainwaves
Pass through time and space.

*

It is
A hostile place
Governed by barbarians
That surround the was
The Truth and the life
As the crystal crow
Enters a moment
Of blind doublespeak.

Pulling the trigger
On the end game
He blasts the center
Of corrupt minds
As the shadows
Of their thoughts
Eat them alive.

As time buries them
In the debris
Of their endeavors
The scarlet rose
Looks to the dawn

Of peace in the face
Of victory.

So
It is freedom
That waves the banner
Of Truth and justice
As the children of promise
Dance in the streets.

So
The Spirit of Wisdom
Guided the scarlet rose
Through a valley
Of dry bones and the life
Of being toward Truth
Endured.

Then
The stones cried out
With a flurry of thanks
And the crystal crow
Advanced time
Into a one-dimensional reality.

Where there was darkness
The sc arlet rose spoke light.

Where there was the cover
Of deception

The crystal crow planted
A garden of splendor
And the blooms blossom
Truth forevermore.

So
Out of chaos and the abyss
Came the trumpet
Of The Unknown God
As the drums of eternity
Carried on.

*

It is
A sad day on the home front
As the spirit
Of a land weeps
And the children of promise
Bury their head in their hands.

So
Grief is not pretty
When justice is not served.

How
The fist of freedom
Raises a flag of deliverance
As the dead ache the life
Of the living.

As the blood
Of the very best
Drenches the sand
Of infamy
Lady Liberty arms herself
With courage and conviction.

There is
A moment of silence
Before she storms
Into battle.

There is
Truth in her heart
As she mounts
Death and destruction
To the barbarians
And time and times
And a half bury them
In a lake of fire.

So
There is a witness
To a tragic end
Of men of valor.

So
The fury of destiny
Defines the moment
As the land

Of the free and brave
Brings home heroes
Of Truth and justice.

As the Truth of freedom
Sets the power
Of Lady Liberty
Against the barbarians
The world salutes her
And the struggle
Of an age bleeds silence.

Then
An anthem of peace and hope
Triumphs over the oppressors.

*

Turning to the way
The Truth and the life
The crystal crow felt
The deep touch
Of The Unknown God
As The Spirit of Wisdom
Embraced him with love.

It was
The entrance to the peace
Beyond understanding
That flourished

In the living moment
As hope carried him
Into the light
Of forevermore.

Then
He engaged the rhythm
Of the universe
Pursuing the mana
Of what matters
And trumpets sounded
Announcing the birth
Of pure music.

As the dawn
Of being toward Truth
Opened thought
To the other side
Of the sky
The crystal crow listened
To the voice of the scarlet rose
And her life gathered
Time and times and a half
Into the living moment.

Deep into meditation
He gazed into the unknown
Finding the touchstone
Of Truth and justice

And his mind pyramided
Onto the drums of eternity.

There was
The pounding
Of the heart
Of forevermore
Defining a passion
For freedom
As the scarlet rose
Danced her way
Into the substance
Of his meat.

As his faith
Carried him out of darkness
He believed himself
Into the light
Of a one-dimensional
Reality.

So
Their brainwaves
Are blowing in the wind.

*

As her brainwaves
Penetrate his substance
Endless possibility arouses

Time and times and a half
Until the intimate connection
Of her deep touch
Speaks an awesome wonder
Into the dawn of his thought.

Then
She pulls the trigger
Of the living moment
As he feels his way
Into the unknown.

Ever deeper into trance
The crystal crow passes
Milestone after milestone
Until he reaches pure music.

Then
The scarlet rose allows
His mind to release
His being toward Truth
From the darkness
Of the abyss
And thoughts explode
Across the horizon
Of the given.

Pulling out of trance
The crystal crow embraces
The living moment

After the wounds of war
Crippled his mind
And the drums of eternity
Carry his thoughts
Onto the rhythm of the universe.

So
Her brainwaves comfort him.

So
He climbs out of himself
Opening his heart
To meet the scarlet rose.

Then
Truth and justice paint
A two-dimensional reality
From his vision of the other side
Of time and space.

So
The celestial clocks
Chime the hour
Of peace beyond
Understanding
As the scarlet rose dances
Into his dreams.

*

Passing across the horizon
Onto the enormity of nothingness
The crystal crow gathers
His strength to endure.

How
The void defines the shadow
Of what matters
As mind awakens
To the dawn of meaning.

So
His purpose
Is to understand.

So
To understand
Requires the presence
Of The Spirit of Wisdom
As thew heart pounds life
Into the living moment.

To be alive
With the way, the Truth
And the life
Is to dwell with what matters
As thoughts leave the dust
Of being and time.

So
The crystal crow believes
Himself into being toward Truth.

Then
The crystal crow reaches
Beyond the living moment
And into the light
Of The Unknown God
As his mind cultivates
The limitations of thought.

Then
Imagining his way
To the persona
Of Truth and justice
He feels the rhythm
Of the universe lift him
Toward the kiss
Of what matters.

So
Imagining his way
Into the wind
From the rhythm
Of the universe
He sails onto the deep touch
Of Truth and justice
Upon wings of destiny

As he reads the brainwaves
Of the always already there.

*

It is
A time to gather stones
And build an altar
To The Unknown God
As the children of promise
Return from war.

Heading south
The geese announce
The approach of winter
And a chill visits
Morning with a wink and nod.

So
The barbarians held
Their ground
In the crusade
Of the twenty-first century
As the sunset
Over the blood of freedom.

So
The barbarians celebrate
The defeat of Lady Liberty

And darkness triumphs
Over light.

So
The shame of defeat
Burdens the moment
After twenty years
Of holding back hatred
And the war against terrorists
Looms strong.

However
There is the underground
Led by the crystal crow
That infiltrates the bastions
Of hate with the way
The Truth and the life
And the banner of freedom
Waves in the heart
Of the children of promise.

Then
The Spirit of Wisdom
Reaches into the heart
Of what life is about
And Lady Liberty advances
Through the brainwaves
Of Truth and justice.

It is
That freedom possesses
The power to bring light
To dark minds and darker hearts
Allowing the mantra
Of live and let live
To bring a lasting peace.

So
War profits the despots
And puppet masters
At the cost of human life.

*

Feeling his way
Through channels of brainwaves
The crystal crow senses
A communique of despots
That threaten life
Liberty and the pursuit of happiness
As a vast darkness covers
The here and now.

As the wind takes
The living moment
Into secret knowledge
Time and space collide
With being and nothingness.

Then
The crystal crow throttles
Into streams of consciousness
And thoughts pound life
Into the blood
Of being toward Truth.

Although reading the brainwaves
Of evil intent
Consumes much energy
The crystal crow wields
Power across life and death
And a vertical column of time
Illuminates the darkness
With the brilliance
Of The Spirit of Wisdom.

Then
Pure music bonds
With the rhythm of the universe
And a trumpet awakens
The here and now
To the way
The Truth and the life.

So
The darkness fades
Into a one-dimensional
Reality and Truth shines

Through the rise
Of what matters.

Then
Thoughts scramble
Into silence
And the mind of the crystal crow
Chases the despots into a vast void.

So
Intercepting the brainwaves
Of evil intent
Allows the children of promise
To conquer the barbarians
And allows freedom
In The Unknown God
To prosper and grow.

*

As visions of the other side
Of the sky carry brainwaves
Into the substance
Of the crystal crow
The scarlet rose emerges
Through the rhythm of the universe
And the unknown rises
With the deep touch.

There is
The army of time
And times and a half
Growing into being toward Truth
And they punctuate
The struggle of being
And nothingness.

Suddenly
Pure music breaks
Into the living moment
As the crystal crow
Walks into fathoms
Of consciousness.

Although the scarlet rose
Opens her inner eye
To life, liberty
And the pursuit
Of happiness
She sees only a thick fog
As the drums of eternity
Define time and space.

So
The crystal crow clears
The way beyond the here and now
As the scarlet rose slips
Into a parabola of time

Pyramiding the way
The Truth and the life.

So
The power of Truth
Bonds them
To The Spirit of Wisdom
And they flow into pure music.

Reaching into the authentic
Article, they follow
An unidentified flying object
Into things in themselves
As what matters leads
To The Unknown God.

Then
Visions awaken
From a deep sleep
As thoughts eclipse
The mind.

SECTION 5

LEAPING OUT OF SELF

As the artist traced
Being and nothingness
To an existential threat
Annabel Lee worked
Life, liberty and the pursuit
Of happiness into the foundation
Of being toward Truth.

It was
The life of freedom
That they configured
In the here and now
Although a sense of presence
Seemed to fall
Into shadows of thought.

How
That happens
Seemed to be
The spaces between
Lines of understanding
An illusion based
On contradiction.

So
The artist found himself
Somewhere between
There and not there
As time poured
The moment into silence

And Annabel Lee composed
Pure music in the sands
Of time.

Then
They ached for clarity
For the fog of what mattered.

Then
They addressed
Their inner eye
To the dawning
Of being toward Truth.

Pyramiding
Through the unknown
They rubbed freedom
Into life as the wind
Carried an understanding
Of the mystery of life.

How
Questions danced
In their mind
As a void threatened
The approach
To their presence.

So
They proceeded

To the other side
Of the sky
As visions took them
Into the rhythm
Of the universe.

Pounding the moment
Into what was there
The artist pictured
A wilderness of thought
Beyond the limitations
Of mind.

Although there are only
Three dimensions
There is a multitude
Of realities.

*

As being toward Truth
Energizes brainwaves
To endless possibility
Through the inner eye
The artist releases images
Portraying the mysteries of life
And pure music becomes
The doctrine of the landscape.

Following the brainwaves
Of the universe
He calls upon the light
Shining from The Spirit of Wisdom
And a one-dimensional reality
Drops into presence.

It is
The unearthing
Of what matters
From the debris
Left by the power mongers
That speaks freedom
Into the moment
As images of Truth grow
From a fertile imagination.

Then
And only then
Annabel Lee imagines
Life across a horizon
Of thought.

As her sweat takes
The artist through a valley
Of dry bones
Images flow with a river
Of beauty
And the beholding

Of the unknown
Becomes a way of life.

It is
The vitality of curiosity
That extends
The experiential
Beyond the limitations
Of being there.

Then
The authentic article
Of presence
Documents the other side
Of time
As the way, the Truth
And the life witnesses
Being toward Truth.

Then
The linear world listens
To The Unknown God
Speak peace beyond
Understanding.

So
The power mongers
Dissolve in the futility
Of their folly
And the children of promise

Restore life, liberty
And the pursuit of happiness.

*

Back from the other side
Of time and space
The artist carves life
Into the living moment
As Annabel Lee gathers
Images from memories
Of her tour of duty.

There are
Splashes of thought
In the wind
As pure music carries
Them into visions
Of what matters.

Then
They connect
To the rhythm
Of brainwaves
Dancing into time
And times and a half.

Then
Passion surges in the blood
And being toward Truth

Arms the moment
With a wave of spirits.

So
Annabel Lee becomes
His touchstone
Bringing light to shadows
Of thought
As the doctrine
Of the landscape
Liberates a rush of feelings
Beyond the experiential.

Then
The center no longer holds.

Then
Frenetic chaos charges
The wind with images
From the other side
Of time and space
And the artist bleeds
The mystery of life
From the celestial clocks
As time drips
Meaning into songs
of power and strength.

So
Annabel Lee advances

Into being and nothingness
With her finger on the trigger
Of the artist's imagination
As spirits
In the living moment
Mold certain Truth.

*

There is
Love in the wind
As the artist braves
The unknown
And the spirits
Of being toward Truth
Carry the passion
For life into pure music.

So
The celebration
Of times and a half
Equips him
With the language
Of splendor
As Annabel Lee covers
The moment with kisses.

Then
He looks to the trail
Of tears

As she speaks of tragedy
And spirits pound
The drums of eternity.

Caught by the Truth
The artist configures
A message
As freedom spirits
The moment with
The authentic article.

As the artist follows
Annabel Lee into the deep touch
An image of the children of promise
An image
Of the children of promise
Marching to their death
Touches him with grief.

Wondering about
The notion of progress
The artist documents
The true history
Written with the blood
Of the past.

Reaching into the heart
That lives in liberty
The artist pictures
A tear in the wind.

Although Truth reveals
The historical past
As a sacrifice
Annabel Lee guides the artist
In a portrayal of the cost
Of the now.

*

There is
A portal to the other side
Of time and space
Founded upon the authentic
Article of being toward Truth
And the artist follows
The muse to launch
Into that beyond.

As the living moment
Expands the here and now
To encompass transcendence
Pure music brings images
Of the unknown
Into brain waves.

Then
The muse feeds him
With a gathering of ideation
Through the exercise
Of his imagination.

So
The dawn of ideation
Opens endless possibility
To the substance
Of what matters
As the brainwaves register
In his thoughts.

So
The muse enables him
To grasp what is there
Through the deep touch.

It is
The essence of thought
That speaks the language
Of Truth to his heart
As he feels his way
Through the unknown
By a leap of faith.

Orchestrating the rhythm
Of the universe
Into distinct points
Of reference
The muse liberates
The artist from the limitations
Of linear reality.

Then
The artist climbs
Out of himself
To bathe in the light
Of a one-dimensional
Reality
As The Spirit of Wisdom
Anoints his being
Toward Truth.

It is
The bond between
The artist and his muse
That allows a sense
Of presence to be.

Presence is the pure music
Of the way, the Truth
And the life
Onto The Unknown God.

*

Sitting beneath
A white oak tree
An old man collects
Brainwaves from the always
Already there.

Journeying
Into the mystery
Of life, he grasps visions
Formed by the drums
Of eternity.

So
The spirits live
Among the living
And the dead
As destiny emits
Brainwaves
Into the rhythm
Of the universe.

They are
The mechanism that liberates
Time and times
And a half, governed
By The Spirit of Wisdom
And through the deep touch.

Traveling through the here
And now, the spirits reflect
The way, the Truth and the life
Into a leap of faith
As the mystery of life grows
From the unknown.

So
The spirits are
The angels of heaven
While the specters
Are the fallen angels
And they war
In the heart and mind.

So
Predestination is only viewed
From a one-dimensional
Reality, while the living
Are confined to linear
Time and space.

How
Meditation allows
The old man
To explore the unknown.

Although grounded
In the actual
Meditation allows
The old man to journey
To the other side
Of time and space
Gaining presence
With The Unknown God.

*

It was
Nine/eleven and thunder
Roared throughout her body
As mind looked at a day
Of infamy.

Echoes
Of nine/eleven pounded
Blood into tears.

It was
the spark that ignited
the crusade
of the twenty-first
century.

Out of darkness
Came an existential threat
And the land of the free
And brave mustered its muscle
To face terrorists.

So
Children of promise
Were brutally attacked
Because they lived for life
Liberty and the pursuit
Of happiness.

So
The next generation
Of the faithful
That must carry the baton
Of freedom and it is
Their duty to defend
Human rights.

So
It is twenty years after
From that very day
That children of promise
Must unite against
The tyranny of darkness.

How
Sad even thinking of surrender.

So
Lady Liberty must stand tall
Equipped with the guns
Of Truth in one hand
And the light of justice
In the other hand.

*

Feeling the energy emitted
From the other side
Of the sky, the artist

Sees into the mystery
Of life and eternity opens
The workings behind
The here and now.

As pure music emerges
Into time and space
The brain waves
Of being toward Truth
Penetrate the living moment
With vibrant images
That liberate mind
From the constraints
Of the dull round.

So
The artist maneuvers
Into the living moment
By riding the rhythm
Of the universe, as the muse
Dances in his mind.

Then
The mystery of life
Colors his thoughts
With a passion for life
Liberty and the pursuit
Of happiness.

So
The doctrine of the landscape
Feeds upon The Spirit
Of Wisdom as the muse
Kisses a song of joy and wonder.

Then
The other side of the sky
Writes Truth and justice
Into the mind of the artist
With the blood of the always
Already there.

How
The artist triumphs
Over darkness
With the light
Of the way, the Truth
And the life.

So
The artist orchestrates
The peace beyond understanding
With the presence
Of The Unknown God.

There are
Spirits in the wind
That endow the artist
With visions.

*

While the artist meditated
He felt spirits of kindness
Around him
Healing his wounds from time past
As pure music took his mind
To the peace beyond understanding.

It was
Bathing in the living moment
With treasures of sensation.

It was
The embracing of a private
Wonder as being was carried off
To splendor and he looked
Into the substance
Of being and nothingness.

As he tuned into
The brainwaves
Of the always already there
He felt the rhythm
Of the universe vitalize
His being toward Truth
And the existential threat
Of a crazed world disappeared
For times and a half.

Then
The artist was equipped
With the strength
To endure the abuse
Of the dull round
As he pressed the terror
Of the barbarians
Into a sad song.

So
The Spirit of Wisdom sent
The spirits of love and devotion
To minister to the artist
As he engaged a vision
Of what matters.

Then
The artist beheld the beauty
Of the living moment
As well as the crude ugliness
Of the barbicans.

So
The way, the Truth
And the life
Taught him the power
Of love wielded
By The Unknown God.

*

As the echoes of pure music
Caress being toward Truth
Annabel Lee extends her mind
Into the always already there
And the artist rides
The rhythm of the universe
To a two-dimensional reality.

Passing milestone after
Milestone in the unknown
He connects to The Spirit
Of Wisdom.

Then
A vision of eternity
Shines on in the darkness
As he opens a testament
Of Truth and she spirits
The pathway through
The mystery of life.

So
Together they reach
Into endless possibility.

As pure music defines
The movement of the actual
Brainwaves pyramid
Spirits into the substance
Of thought.

Suddenly
The wickedness of the barbarians
Attack the foundation
Of life, liberty
And the pursuit of happiness.

Believing herself
Into the living moment
Annabel Lee brings
The deep touch into focus
As a lost generation
Squanders hope.

As the dignity
Of the children of promise
Bends to the will
Of specters
The way, the Truth
And the life speaks
Power and strength.

Then
Annabel Lee dances
At the edge of thought.

So
Time and times
And a half cancel
The corrupt
As the children of promise

Follow the presence
Of The Unknown God.

*

Driven by the winds
Of the immediate
As dark magic surrounds
The living moment
The artist does not
Back down.

Confronted with his mortality
While barbarians wield
Swords of infamy
The artist stands tall
Upon the conviction
Of his heart.

It is
Life, liberty and the pursuit
Of happiness
That carries him
From one now point
To another
Because death had
No dominion.

As his vision
Of what matters

Focuses upon the way
The Truth and the life
He composers an image
Of power and strength
And the world trembles.

In his message
The light of The Spirit
Of Wisdom shines
With Truth and justice
As individual freedom
Awakens a song
Of independence.

So
Annabel Lee summons
The spirits, those angels
Of heaven
To equip the artist
With the courage
To endure and to conquer
Dark magic with pure music.

Extending an anthem
Of hopes and dreams
From the everlasting
She defends the rights
Of the living
As The Spirit of Wisdom
Infuses a right spirit

Into the breath
Of the living.

Then
Annabel Lee dances
Liberty into the wind
Upon wings of the always
Already there
As The Unknown God smiles.

*

Buried in the heart
Of what matters
The will of being toward Truth
Trumpets the vision of the artist
As his muse, Annabel Lee
Carries his thoughts
Beyond the pale.

It is
The dawn of survival
In his mind.

It is
The anthem of hope
That sings in the void.

As the artist empties
His critical mass

In times and a half
He feels the warmth
Of his muse spirit
His labored breath.

So
He endures the turmoil
Of being and nothingness.

So
The wounds upon his mind
Leave scars to remind him
Of his struggle to be

When alone in the darkness
Of ignominy
Confronted by peril
He looks to The Spirit of Wisdom.

So
He endures the trauma
Surrounding him.

With a passion
He heads toward the way
The Truth and the life.

Then
He wills himself through faith
To paint the living moment.

So
To know Truth
And to conquer the void
He reaches beyond thought
To the meaning
Of the everlasting.

Piling millstone upon millstone
He builds an altar
To The Unknown God
Meditating upon his purpose
In the here and now
And finding the
peace beyond understanding.

So
He pictures a cry of tears.

*

There is
A sadness in the air
That confounds the mind.

As the living moment
Collides with nothingness
Emptiness compounds
The struggle in being
Toward Truth.

The existential threat
Of the void cripples thought
As the artist listens
To the cry of the doctrine
Of the landscape.

To advance
Beyond the immediate
Seems futile
Because alternate realities
Appear delusional
As the actual dominates
The here and now.

To escape
Dread defines want
In the language
Of self-preservation.

Then
The artist faces the void
With trepidation
As he musters the courage
To confront
The madness of the world.

It is
The death of meaning
And the tyranny

Of nothingness
That devours time present.

To console him
His muse pyramids
Pure music into his heart
As time and space register
The pulse of hope.

Then
The artist feels
A good measure of love
From The Unknown God
As his muse caresses
His mind
With what matters.

Gathering his wits
He feels his will return
To the way, the Truth
And the life
As The Spirit of Wisdom
Heals his wounded mind.

*

As the artist
Approaches his composition
He sees beyond the here and now

And his muse articulates
The mystery of life into his blood.

There is
The stirring of brainwaves
Into his vision
Equipping him with an image
Beneath the surface
Of being and time.

How
His thoughts spin
An entrance into the substance
Of life
And he hears pure music
Take his mind
Into an overture of blues.

From his presence
Comes the brainwaves
Of being toward Truth.

Following the rhythm
Of the universe, he connects
To the other side
Of time and space
While his muse
Undresses his reality.

Then
Annabel Lee takes
The artist into the center
Of what matters
And she opens his thoughts
To endless possibility.

Hearing life empty
The living moment
The artist reaches
Into the light
Of a one-dimensional
Reality
As the point
Of his composition
Feels understanding.

So
the artist conquers
dark silence
with the substance
of what matters
and the brainwaves
of the virtual are formed
from illusion
the deception in perception.

So
The artist sees the way

Through the unknown
In his work.

It is
A picture of understanding.

*

It was
A time beyond
The here and now
That the muse
Took the artist
Into the mystery of life
And visions of pure music
Seeded his mind
With the deep touch.

Far into the unknown
She took him
As the rhythm
Of the universe defined
The living moment.

Then
A mass of spirits trumpeted
What matters into his vision
As he opened
His inner eye to life, liberty
And the pursuit of happiness.

It was
The anthem of freedom
That echoed into his being
Toward Truth
And his muse danced
Light into darkness.

Believing himself
Into the way, the Truth
And the life
The artist grasped
An image of the always
Already there
And his sight filled
With The Spirit of Wisdom.

Sensing a reality
Moving into his heart
The artist saw
Through a looking glass
To visions of splendor
As the muse orchestrated
Pure presence, a melody
Of peace and hope.

Then
The doctrine of the landscape
Pictured the living moment
With bloody meat
And Annabel Lee drove

The mystery of life
Into his substance.

So
He was with her
Through the muscle
Of endless possibility
As the portrait
Of being and nothingness
Covered the void.

*

From the depths
Of the unknown
A vision stirred
Awakening the artist
To the mystery of life.

It was
The source of the rhythm
Of the universe.

It was
The pulse of a one
Dimensional reality.

As the light
Of the always already
There opened thought

To the life
Of being toward Truth
Pure music took the artist
Beyond the here and now
And into the elements
Of what matters.

Then
Blind want consumed
Him with the passion
For understanding
As The Spirit of Wisdom
Filled him
With the authentic
Article.

Easing back into the here
And now, his mind traced
An image of splendor
As need opened
His third eye to the way
The Truth and the life.

Believing himself
Into the always already
There, the artist
Intercepted the brainwaves
Of being and nothingness
As the substance

Of life danced dreams
Into his presence.

Then
He addressed the actual.

Then
He lanced being and time.

As the light of forevermore
Creased his vision
He knelt before
The Unknown God.

So
There is life
To being toward Truth
That transcends understanding.

*

Summoning the will to be
An old man crawled into the dawn
Of what matters
As time wound down to oblivion.

It was
That he did not fear death
But saw it

As a miracle for service
To The Unknown God.

It was
That the vigor he once had
Left him.

Standing at the edge
Of the void
He looked at his face
And saw a life of victory.

Having explored the unknown
Through his life
The old man rested his eyes
On the dance of wonder.

So
He listened to the drums
Of eternity and followed
The rhythm of the universe.

Then
He felt the authentic article
Write the mystery of life
Onto his heart.

So
The old man bathed

In the peace
Beyond understanding.

Then
The breath of life
Took him
On another journey
Into the unknown
Opening his heart
To the way, the Truth
And the life.

Although a song
Liberated his mind
His meat was weak
But he muscled up
His will
As The Spirit of Wisdom
Infused into his substance
The living moment.

So
The old man continues on.

*

Connecting to the brainwaves
From the other side
Of time and space
The artist drew

The mystery of life
Into the living moment.

As the muse turned
His inner eye
Onto endless possibility
He willed himself
Through a looking glass
Into life, liberty and the pursuit
Of happiness.

Although he was free
From bondage
To the here and now
He retained a foothold
In the actual
As his mind carried
Upon being toward Truth.

Then
A multitude of brainwaves
Bombarded his thought
As he pictured
The blood of pure music.

Then
He projected brainwaves
To the other side
Of time and space

As pure music defined
What matters.

So
The one dimensional
Reality surfaced
With the light
Of the always
Already there.

From The Spirit of Wisdom
He grasped the drift
Of purpose as his will
Impassioned being toward
Truth to carry
His brainwaves into the rhythm
Of the universe.

Then
Time trumpeted
Into song
As space formed
A two-dimensional
Reality
And the artist
Painted the wind
With the drums
Of eternity.

*

Then
The dark magic
Of the specters
Surrounded the artist
With thoughts of deception
And he fought
With all his might
To rebuke
This sinister scheme.

As the blood
Of madness clogged
His understanding
The spirits, those angels
Of heaven fought
This intrusion.

It was
The war of principalities
Waged in the heart
Of being toward Truth
As the brainwaves
From the other side
Of time and space
Triggered his will to be
And the spirits plunged
A consuming torch
Into the midst
Of the specters

Cancelling the power
Of dark magic.

It was
The artist's freedom
Was in jeopardy.

It was
That he would not
Surrender to the deception
Set by the powermongers.

Drinking in power
Of the way, the Truth
And the life
The artist engulfed
The demigods in flames
Of pure music
And The Spirit
Of Wisdom pyramided
The dark magic
Into the dry places
Of oblivion.

To defeat
The dark magic
Of deception
Took the power
Of The Spirit of Wisdom

Working through
The artist's faith.

Crippled by the love
Of The Unknown God
The specters were
Vanquished.

*

With the source
Of his brainwaves
In the interstices of mind
Being toward Truth
Emits images of pure music
And the artist projects
His substance into a two
Dimensional reality.

Although the existential
Threat of being there
Attempts to block
His brainwaves
The rhythm of the universe
Supports the integrity
Of the artist.

As he looks
At the palm at the end
Of mind, his muse

Orchestrates the substance
Of his being toward Truth
And the horizon
Of the living moment
Explodes into presence.

Then
The celestial clocks strike
The here and now
With actuality, and the living
Moment caresses
His brain waves
Onto forevermore.
While the artist rifles
Images into the beyond
His muse directs him
To the way, the Truth
And the life.

It is
The song of The Spirit
Of Wisdom that escalates
Him into endless possibility
As his muse shines
Truth and justice
Into the shadows
Of dark magic.

Then
A lone cry for life

Shatters the living moment
And the muse dispels
The greed for power.

So
There is strength
In the muscle of Truth
And justice.

So
The artist applies
His faith in The Unknown
God to the calculus
Of what matters.

*

Drunk on pain
The artist formed
A vision of the other side
Of time and space
A one-dimensional reality
When The Spirit of Wisdom
Opened his heart
To the way, the Truth
And the life.

There was
The presence of majesty
Through the look

Of being toward Truth
As his mind
Probed the unknown
And the mystery of life
Spilled blood
Across the landscape
Of mind.

Although crippled
With pain
He saw hope
Through his faith
In The Unknown God
As he suffered
Through his affliction.

As he registered
The brainwaves
Of Truth and justice
Pure music took him
Into the elements
Of what matters.

So
He pictured the house
Of many mansions
As the other side
Of time and space
And it was the presence
Of a one-dimensional

Reality
The light of the always
Already there
On the other side
Of the here and now.

Picking himself up
From his pain
He portrayed
The living moment
As entrance
Into life, liberty
And the pursuit
Of happiness.

As his brainwaves
Traveled across the horizon
His muse spirited
His thoughts
Into the everlasting.

So
The drums
Of eternity pyramided
The rhythm of the universe
Into the here and now
And pure music danced
The living moment
Into his life.

So
The muse bound
His wounds
Easing his pain.

SECTION 6

ABOVE GROUND

Channeling the brainwaves
From the unknown
Annabel Lee sought
The elements of what matters
And the blue of the blue
Sky covered
The landscape of the here
And now with hope.

It was
A time when the spirits
Of heaven danced
Across the horizon
Of mind, as thoughts
Gathered traces
To the mystery of life.

Although the children
Of promise were eager
To hear the pure music
Of a one-dimensional
Reality
They waited at the edge
Of the frontier.

To be filled
With the certain love
Of The Unknown God
They looked to guidance
From The Spirit of Wisdom

For the way, the Truth
And the life.

So
The dreams of the children
Of promise could be filled
With the desire
For Truth and justice
The defining energy
Of what matters.

Into the encompassing
Of the blue sky
Annabel Lee took
The children of promise
With visions
Of endless possibility
Where they saw
The dance of the rhythm
Of the universe.

It was
An epiphany
A magnitude beyond
Time and space
As the pulse
Of a one-dimensional
Reality fed life, liberty
And the pursuit of happiness
To their being toward Truth.

So
The spirits of heaven
Brought splendor
To their living moment.

*

So
It was the children
Of promise constituted
The muscle of the militia
That preserved and protected
Lady Liberty.

They were unmatched
As a global force
In the protection of life
Liberty and the pursuit
Of happiness.

When engaged in battle
They had singular
Unified focus: to win.

Filled with the passion
Of pure music, they
Trumpeted the barbarians
Into death and destruction.

So
The crystal crow and Annabel Lee
Led the fight
Crushing the barbarians
And bleeding the demigods
Dry, as the crusade
Of the 21st century
Erupted with the advance
Of terrorism.

It was
That the barbarians
Were determined
To dominate the world
With their ideology.

They had no tolerance
For the freedom
Of the individual
And they viewed
Life, liberty
And the pursuit of happiness
As a grievous evil.

Trusting The Spirit
Of Wisdom
The children pf promise
Headed across the terrain
In their hunt
For the demigods

Who were possessed
By specters.

The children of promise
Only wanted to live
And let live
With the freedom
Of human rights
As their inheritance.

So
With the strength
Of Truth and justice
Lady Liberty stared
Down the enemy.

*

Following the brain waves
From the unidentified
Flying objects
The children of promise
Opened their hearts
To the authentic article
As pure music gave them
A sense of duty to Lady Liberty.

It was
The freedom of being
Toward Truth

That intensified their will
To face the demigods
And battle the barbarians.

It was
Their faith in The Unknown
God that brought them
To the threshold
Of this existential threat
Because life, liberty
And the pursuit
Of happiness was
Their destiny.

So
War is the brutal cruelty
That the children
Of promise endured.

Equipped with fists of fire
They advanced across time
And space, throttling
The barbarians into oblivion.

As the madness
Of the barbarians
Attacked Lady Liberty
She stood strong
With the courage

Of harden steel
In her muscle.

Allied with the puppet
Masters of the world
The barbarians fed hate
Into time and times
And a half, as this
New crusade dominated
The dull round.

It took a full measure
Of time to eradicate
The puppet masters
Because they sold
Their ideology
To the barbarians.

So
The twenty-first century
Was sold to a new crusade.

*

Although his mind
Was surrounded by dark
Magic, the crystal crow fought
His way to life, liberty
And the pursuit of happiness.

So
He would not surrender
His being toward Truth
And he called
Upon The Spirit of Wisdom
To guide him into the peace
Beyond understanding.

As the children
Of promised shined
The light of the way
The Truth and the life
Upon his thought
The crystal crow was delivered
From his trepidation.

So
The specters
Of the demigods
Retreated to the shadows
Of being and time
As the signature
Of the scarlet rose
Sealed them away.

Leaving the abyss behind
The crystal crow felt
The energy of pure music
Restore his substance
As the one-dimensional

Reality attuned his being
Toward Truth through
The mystery of life.

Then
The children of promise
Gathered in the garden
Of tables and chairs
To reload.

They prepared the fatted calf
To celebrate
The return of the crystal crow.

It was
A moment when
The scarlet rose danced
Joy and wonder
In the presence
Of The Unknown God.

Then
They all knelt
In silent prayer
With thankful hearts.

*

It was
An invasion of deceit

By the demigods
That prompted
The unidentified
Flying objects to signal
Lady Liberty to make ready
For the fight for freedom
And the celestial clocks
Configured the destiny
Of life, liberty, and the pursuit
Of happiness.

For the children of promise
It was a call to duty.

So
They gathered in the valley
Of dry bones
With the gear of warriors
Fully armed for battle.

Then
The sun rose
With a thirst for blood.

It was
Off to the front lines
And pulling the trigger
On the despots
In defense of Lady Liberty.

Eclipsing the here and now
The children of promise
Marched into battle
As the UFOs
Covered the landscape
With the scent of victory.

So
They followed the rhythm
Of the universe
Reaching into their faith
In the power
Of a one-dimensional
Reality.

As time passed
The earth erupted
In a thunder blast
And the world fell
To its knees.

Leading the integrity
Of the individual
Lady Liberty struck
The puppet masters
With the muscle
Of eternity
And the children
Of promise bludgeoned

The specters
With Truth and justice.

*

Although his mind awoke
To the dawn
Of the no longer, he stepped
Into the other side
Of the here and now
Until he felt the rhythm
Of the universe feed
His brainwaves
The substance of life.

It was
The war of principalities
That pulled the trigger
On what matters.

Then
The old man found
His way to the authentic
Article and his dreams
Flourished
In the living moment.

Because he would not
Surrender to the dark magic
Of the demigods

And their specters
He fed on the light
Of a one-dimensional
Reality.

So
He built a reality
Founded upon the way
The Truth and the life.

As he passed the mystery
Of life through thoughts
And dreams
He found the energy
To endure
Through the ache
Of being and nothingness.

Although the void
Of the no longer
Was there, he followed
The Spirit of Wisdom
To forevermore
And he felt pure music
Endow him
With the breath of life.

Then
The old man accepted
The unidentified flying

Objects as spirits
From heaven.

Then
The deep touch
Of the always already
There wrote his name
In The Book of Life.

So
He thanked The Unknown God
For his deliverance.

*

Although there are
Only three dimensions
There is a vast multitude
Of realities but only one
Actuality, only one
Veritable presence.

It is
The defining rubric
Of time and space
As written in the law
Of what matters.

So
Mind orchestrates life

Through being and nothingness
Proceeding onto the living
Moment as thoughts gather
Around core beliefs.

Then
Pure music nourishes
The living moment
Onto epiphany
As the way the Truth
And the life opens
Thought beyond what
Is there.

Then
Through the deep touch
The Spirit of Wisdom
Infuses a pure heart
And a clear mind
As being toward Truth
Grows close to a one
Dimensional reality
A vertical column of time.

So
The light of the always
Already there allows
The breath

In the living moment
To be, as the rhythm
Of the universe carries life.

As time and space presents
The here and now
Mind applies the doctrine
Of the landscape
Into the rubric beyond
The limitations
Of being and time.

Then
The heart believes itself
Onto the threshold
Of forevermore
Praising the awesome
Wonder
Of The Unknown God.

*

As nothingness consumed
The living moment
An old man turned
To The Spirit of Wisdom
For guidance.

Finding a trace
To the way, the Truth

And the life liberated him
From the darkness
Of the abyss
Bring the light
Of the one-dimensional
Reality.

There was
Pure music pouring
Into his substance
Restoring his hopes
And dreams.

Then
He rode upon the rhythm
Of the universe
Through the mystery
Of life until he felt
The deep touch of love
From The Unknown God
And there he dwelt.

There was
An unearthing
Of what matters
That was buried
By nothingness
As he believed his way
Into the presence
Of The Great I am.

To serve
The Unknown God
Was his destiny.

To follow
The way, the Truth
And the life
Liberated him
From the clutches
Of the void.

So
Pure music defined his purpose.

Then
The old man formed
A more perfect union
Establishing the ground
Of Truth and justice.

Then
The children of promi8se
Danced with the doctrine
Of the landscape.

*

Falling into the abyss
An old man cried out

For deliverance
As time exploded
Into times and a half.

There was
The sound of fire
Crackling through times
As his mind spun
Wildly uncontrolled.

He felt the heat
Of despair fry his heart.

Watching his demise
The puppet masters laughed
At the futility
Of the old man
As he was driven down
Into burning embers.

There was
Suffering in that time
That surpassed understanding
As he trembled delirious.

He felt beyond hope.

So
The devastation of a soul
And the delirium

In being profoundly lost
Echoed across time and space
As the old man wept blood.

Then
He heard pure music.
Then
He felt the deep touch
Of The Spirit of Wisdom.

Then
He saw the way
The Truth and the life.

Teetering at the brink
Of nothingness and the edge
Of a lake of fire
The old man received
The love
Of The Unknown God
And he was given reprieve.

So
There is Truth and justice
Mercy and deliverance
For the lost
With hope through faith.

*

Stepping out
Of meditation
An old man left
The looking glass
Of the mystery of life
And opened his mind
To actuality
And the brainwaves
Of actuality dwelt
As presence
In the here and now.

Among the sounds
Of what was there
He heard the cries
Of the children of promise
As the dull round pounded
Suffering as their way of life.

Littering the streets
The hopeless bleed
Their lost lives
Deeper into the void
As tycoons drive
Their trinkets
Over the waste.

It is
The greed for power
And the lust for money

That has corrupted
The land of the free
And the brave.

Then
The old man summoned
The children of promise
To the garden of tables
And chairs, and there
He raised the banner
Of stars and stripes.

Asking The Spirit of Wisdom
To fortify the remnant
With power and strength
The old man freed
Lady Liberty from the grip
Of the puppet masters.

Through being toward Truth
He pyramided the way
The Truth and the life
Across the home
Of the free and brave.

Then
The children of promise
Were anointed with pure hearts

And clear minds
As The Unknown God blessed them.

So
Lady Liberty is alive and well.

SECTION 7

READING BRAINWAVES

The shelves in the library
Are empty and together
The scarlet rose and the crystal crow
Weep in the shadows
As flames consume
The knowledge gathered
Across time past.

There is
A deadly silence in the air
Because music no longer
Is allowed.

So
Even the song sparrow
Has been silenced
As bodies of hope
Rot beneath the dogma
Of the here and now.

Wading through the debris
Of consciousness
Mind drowns in the waste
As a sea of blood
Fills the lungs with terror.

So
The barbarians have deleted
Life, liberty and the pursuit
Of happiness from the language.

To be
Obedient is all there is.
Infiltrating the darkness
Of what is there
A trace of light opens
Endless possibility
As the scarlet rose
And the crystal crow
Hide in a wilderness
Of thought.

Then
They pass through
A valley of dry bones
As the sun scorches life
And the curses of barbarians
Blister the living moment
But that trace of light
Is from a one-dimensional
Reality, instilling freedom
Into the dreams
Of the children of promise.

Although the barbarians
Have stolen time present
The way, the Truth and the life
Carries the rhythm of the universe
Into the hearts
Of the children of promise

As the scarlet rose
And the crystal crow
Escape from the ruins of captivity.

*

As mind travels
Beyond the horizon
Of time, being toward Truth
Drinks in the living moment
As the scarlet rose looks
To the one-dimensional
Reality and the crystal crow
Believes what matters
Into his heart.

Suddenly
The sky disappears
As life becomes a curse
Of the barbarians
And they bury Truth
Into the never was.

Then
The anatomy
Of the mystery of life
Appears in the window
Of the always already
There, and the crystal crow

Reads the message
From eternity.

So
The barbarians have canceled
The here and now.

So
All of what is left
Witnesses the death
Of Truth.

Equipped with the connection
To the deep touch through
The inner eye
The scarlet rose pyramids
Purpose into the heart
Of the children of promise
As the crystal crow speaks
Substance in the language
Of forevermore.

When the barbarians attacked
The Spirit of Wisdom
The Unknown God anointed
The scarlet rose
And the crystal crow
With the power of the always
Already there as they pronounced
The living Truth into the actual.

So
The barbarians crumbled
Into dust as the children
Of promise followed the way
The Truth and the life
Into joy and wonder.

*

So
The artist looked
To the other side
Of time and space
Searching for the trigger
To explode a concept of images.

It was
His desire to frame
Endless possibility
Into a now point
Releasing images
Of what matters.

Leaving the here and now
He leaped into the rhythm
Of the universe
As pure music filled
The air with splendor.

Breathing in the substance
Of the living moment
He reached the edifice
Of his muse and she smiled
With devotion in her heart.

There was
The mystery of untold treasures
As time and times
And a half presented
The presence of The Spirit of Wisdom
As the realities that were there
Spoke to his heart.

As he felt
The presence of the way
The Truth and the life
His muse colored
His vision with the light
Of the one-dimensional
Reality and she danced
To pure music
Onto the essential elements
Of being toward Truth.

The artist followed her
Through the looking glass
Of endless possibility.

Trumpeting the presence
Of The Unknown God
The muse showered
The artist with life
Liberty and the pursuit
Of happiness
The wonder of Lady Liberty.

So
Being toward Truth is
The first born of Lady Liberty.

*

As the world spun
Wildly uncontrolled
The scarlet rose held
Onto first principles
As Lady Liberty was
Assaulted in the avenues
Of time and space.

Blind to Truth and justice
Wave upon wave of atrocities
By the barbarians
Intended to destroy
The land of the free
And the brave.

It was
The carnage of the children
Of promise
That cried out in streets
Of misery
Covering the authentic
Article with refuse.

Although the mind took
To life, liberty and the pursuit
Of happiness
The heart felt the pain
Of Lady Liberty
And the death of freedom.

Among the calculous
Of being and time
Are the deconstructions
Of Truth and justice
Provoking the scarlet rose
To engage the spirits
From the other side
Of darkness.

There was
Death and destruction
Of what matters
As the barbarians struck
The integrity
Of being toward Truth

And rivers of blood
Fed the abyss.

So
The spirits listened
To her pleas and answered
Her call
As The Unknown God directed
The physics
Of being and nothingness.

So
The scarlet rose followed
The way, the Truth
And the life
Shielding Lady Liberty
From certain extinction.

*

Inside the interstices
Of mind brainwaves
The other side of existence
Triggered visions of Lady Liberty
Triumphing over darkness
With the light of freedom.

It was
The preeminence of being
Toward Truth

That reached into a one
Dimensional reality
To secure the way, the Truth
And the life among
The children of promise.

So
The thought of the light
Of freedom released
The energy of cataclysmic
Brainwaves that reached
From the other side
Of time and space.

Then
The presence
Of The Unknown God
Pronounced the eternal light
Onto the inner eye
Of being toward Truth
And The Spirit of Wisdom
Celebrated the fortification
Of Truth and justice.

So
The scarlet rose felt
The power of all
And everything
As treasures of thought
Imaged Lady Liberty

Carrying the living moment
Onto forevermore.

Traveling over the edge
Of the universe
The scarlet rose signaled
The beginning of what matters
And the celestial clocks
Moved the hour of times
And a half into the here
And now.

Then
The brainwaves of the always
Already there pyramided
The spirit of Lady Liberty
Into the hearts and minds
Of the children of promise.

As Lady Liberty danced
In the interstices of mind
A multitude of legions
Of the faithful, past and present
Marching into the bastions
Of darkness with the light
Of freedom.

*

Following the way, the Truth
And the life into the one
Dimensional reality
The crystal crow reached
The deep touch of the always
Already there and pure music
Exploded endless possibility
Into a vertical column of time.

As the visions of the other side
Of the here and now presented itself
The celestial clocks issued
Eternity into the spirit.

It was
Taking the substance
Of his will into an overture
Of eternal presence
As the house
Of many mansions rose
Into the doctrine
Of the landscape.

Orbiting around pure music
The crystal crow felt the peace
Beyond understanding.

Then
The living moment
Multiplied the magnitude

Of being toward Truth.

Suddenly
the Spirit of Wisdom
reads forevermore
into his mind
as he leaped outside
of himself.

There was
A treasure in times
And a half that configured
His destiny as a warrior
Of The Unknown God.

So
The mechanics
Of the living moment
Constructed a bridge
To the beyond
And the crystal crow
Channeled the image
Of what was there
Into pure presence.

Returning to the actual
The ground of phenomenal
Reality, he carried Truth
And justice in his heart.

So
He left the shadows
Of being and time.

*

It was
That pure music embraced
The living moment with the peace
Beyond understanding
And the scarlet rose envisioned
The face of endless possibility.

Accessing the other side
Of the here and now she
Opened her heart to The Spirit
Of Wisdom, as the rhythm
Of the universe
Reset the calculus of times
And a half.

Well into a two
Dimensional reality
She saw the doctrine
Of the landscape throw
Stars into the heavens
As the pounding
Of the eternal drums
Pronounced presence
With The Unknown God.

Then
A legion of angels
From heaven directed
Life, liberty and the pursuit
Of happiness
Into the living moment.

It was
The will to be
That gathered the children
Of promise
As the light of a one
Dimensional reality
Surrounded all and everything.

So
The origin of what is
Bled Truth into his substance
Of being toward Truth
Fortifying freedom as the meat
Of what matters.

Appearing in the looking
Glass of the mystery
Of life, a message unearthed
The breath of Lady Liberty.

Then
The barbarians crumbled

Beneath the magnitude
Of what matters.

Although being and nothingness
Spoke confusion
Across times and a half
A remnant of warriors
Advanced into the existential
Threat of being and time.

*

Among a myriad
Of realities
The deep touch leads
To connectivity
As the brain waves
Of the always already there
Orchestrate pure music
Into mind.

Drawing upon the energy
In the will to be
The artist focuses
Upon the rhythm
Of the universe
As he leaves actuality.

To grasp the calculus
Of the mystery of life

He leaps into being
Toward Truth
From the doctrine
Of being and time.

Then
Visions of the other side
Of time and space
Present a language
Of endless possibility
As the artist invests trust
In The Spirit of Wisdom
And images of what is there
Become veritable presence.

It is
The signature of the way
The Truth and the life
That liberates him
From the constraints
Of linearity
As he sees the face
Of what matters.

Then
The artist forms the body
Of Truth and justice.

As the artist bathes
In endless possibility

His mind is clear
And his heart is pure
As he documents
The living moment
When the celestial clocks
Register destiny
Into time and times
And a half.

Although grounded
In the here and now
He travels through a parabola
Of time onto the threshold
Of a one-dimensional reality
As The Unknown God
Calls him from the darkness
Into the light
Of a vertical column of time.

*

Searching
For the origin of Truth
The artist rides
The rhythm of the universe
Through the mystery of life
As the unknown explodes
Into endless possibility.

From the other side
Of the here and now
Pure music pyramids
The Spirit of Wisdom
Into the living moment
And the light
Of the always already there
Shines through the looking glass
Of the inner eye.

Although clouds cover
The immediate
The artist feels his way
Through things in themselves.

Then
Actuality connects mind
To visions of eternity
The domain of what matters.

Although shadows conceal
What is there
The drums of eternity
Allow the signature
Of presence.

Then
The artist figures the calculus
Of being and nothingness.

So
He follows the way
The Truth and the life
Into the heart
Of what is there
As his thoughts
Unearth the substance
Of being toward Truth.

It isa
The pure music
From the beyond
That trumpets his search
Into the chambers
Of a house of many mansions.

Suddenly
Actuality pronounces
The nearness
Of Truth and justice
As time chimes his entrance
Into the domain of Truth.

So
It is that The Unknown God
Is the source of Truth.

*

As the dawn
Of the way, the Truth
And the life pyramids
Light into hopes and dreams
The scarlet rose opens
The world to what matters
And the crystal crow celebrates
The love of The Unknown God.

There is
Truth and justice
In the air, as pure music
Liberates minds and hearts
From the darkness
Of a dark world.

Then
Time and times and a half
Drink in The Spirit
Of Wisdom
And the children of promise
Conquer the existential threat
Of the puppet masters
Spoken in the language
Of being and nothingness.

How
The war of principalities
Proves Lady Liberty
Victorious.

So
The artist sings
Truth and justice
In radiant colors.

Then
The scarlet rose grasps
The geometry
Of time and space
As the crystal crow marches
Into life forevermore.

Leaving behind the abyss
That encapsulates the world
They form
A more perfect union
Out of a valley of dry bones.

Speaking the language
Of Truth and justice
The scarlet rose
Connects to a one
Dimensional reality
As The Unknown God
Liberates the children of promise
With joy and wonder.

How
The love of The Unknown God
Surpasses understanding.

So
The world awakens
To the mystery of life
With a clear mind
And a pure heart.

*

Riding the rhythm
Of the universe
Into the unknown
The scarlet rose found a trace
To the other side
Of time and space
As the light of a one
Dimensional reality shone
Upon the way, the Truth
And the life.

It was
The Spirit of Wisdom
That showered her
With the sound of pure music
As she felt the deep touch
Of the mystery of life.

Then
The crystal crow saw
Her dissolve into being
Toward Truth

As he stepped with her
Into another reality.

Among the splendor
Of what was there
Mountains rushed
Into the sea
And torrents of clouds
Covered the doctrine
Of the landscape.

It was
A vision of the house
Of many mansions
That exploded their minds
As the drums
Of eternity pronounced
Presence.

Then
The scarlet rose pyramided
Being and nothingness
Into the blood
Of being toward Truth
And the crystal crow
Gathered the living moments
With a vertical column
Of time.

As the energy
From the other side
Of time and space
Connected to her brainwaves
The horizon grew
Into a rhapsody of passion
And the crystal crow wrote
The signature
Of what matters.

So
Together, they witnessed
The presence
Of The Unknown God.

*

As mind unearths Truth
Heart pounds the living moment
Into being toward Truth
And the brainwaves
From the other side
Of time and space infuse
The rhythm of the universe
Into presence.

So the scarlet rose envisions
The face of endless possibility
As the crystal crow connects
To a one-dimensional reality.

Then
Times and a half
Escape from being
And nothingness
As the void is consumed
By the mystery of life.

Focusing her understanding
On the way, the Truth
And the life, the scarlet rose
Connects to The Spirit
Of Wisdom
As the crystal crow
Anchors his inner eye
Onto life, liberty
And the pursuit
Of happiness.

There is
The stirring of an enigma
In the looking glass
Of the mystery of life
And pure music liberates
The moment from the linear time.

So
It is that the scarlet rose
Travels through being and time
As the crystal crow
Seeks the doctrine

Of the landscape.

As the dawn of faith
Opens the gates
To a house
Of many mansions
Thought registers the brainwaves
Of blessed assurance
And life breathes
The authentic article
Into being toward Truth.

To
Own into being toward Truth
Allows the scarlet rose
To dwell in the presence
Of The Unknown God
As the crystal crow follows
The way, the Truth
And the life
Into what matters.

Printed in the United States
by Baker & Taylor Publisher Services